Bringing Up Baby

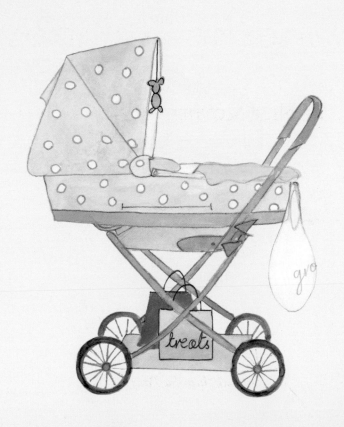

Bringing Up Baby

THE NEW MOTHERS' COMPANION

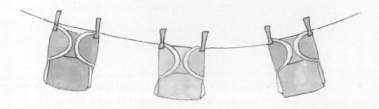

Daisy Goodwin

with Tabitha Potts

HODDER &
STOUGHTON

This book is published to accompany the television series
Bringing Up Baby, produced for Channel 4 by
Silver River Productions Limited and first broadcast in 2007.

First published in Great Britain in 2007 by Hodder & Stoughton
An Hachette Livre UK company

1

A CIP catalogue record for this title is available from the British Library.

ISBN 978-0-340-93623-8

Design by Lisa Pettibone
Typeset in Adobe Garamond and Lucida Handwriting

Illustrati   2007

Every i   ship
of the co   it may
have occu   ditions

Hodder ¡   wable
and recycl   forests.
The loggi   to the

Hodder & Stoughton Ltd
A division of Hodder Headline
338 Euston Road
London NW1 3BH

www.hodder.co.uk

~ Contents

INTRODUCTION 6

CHAPTER 1

Nine Months Inside 8

CHAPTER 2

And Now The Fun Begins 46

CHAPTER 3

Food For Thought 80

CHAPTER 4

And So To Bed 120

CHAPTER 5

Bottoms And Burps 154

CHAPTER 6

Raising The Perfect Child 184

CHAPTER 7

Girls And Boys Come Out To Play 220

CHAPTER 8

The Hand That Rocks The Cradle 252

ACKNOWLEDGEMENTS 286

PICTURE CREDITS 287

~Introduction

When I was pregnant with my first child I must have consumed my ever-increasing body weight in baby books. It was the biggest thing that had ever happened to me so it made sense to do my research. In the early 1990s Penelope Leach was my bible. Following her lead I tried to be mindful of my baby's burgeoning identity. I even avoided *The Archers* because she thought listening to speech radio was tantamount to ignoring your child.

Ten years later I was a mother again, and discovered that I had forgotten everything – even how to change a nappy! I was straight on to Amazon to get help. One of my friends recommended *The Contented Little Baby Book* by Gina Ford. In my post-partum daze I was grateful for its timetables and the sense it gives its readers that babies can be mastered. Of course, everything in the book makes sense on the page, but I found it impossible to follow its advice in real life. I am full of admiration for those mothers, like my youngest sister, who have routines and stick to them; who put their babies down for a nap and pick them up smiling and refreshed two hours later. No amount of well-meaning advice could make me that kind of mother. If my daughter cried when I put her down I tried very hard not to pick her up, but I always caved in. In the end I found my old copy of Penelope Leach and read that. Soppy old attachment theorist she might be, and tough on talk radio, but at least she didn't make me feel guilty about cuddling my baby when she cried.

I was lucky that as a second-time mother I had already learnt the most important lesson: that a baby is born with its own personality, its likes and dislikes, and its energy levels, and there isn't much you can do about it. I think the reason some parents swear by the recent spate of baby-fascist books is that they are the sort of people who love routines and their babies have inherited their love of order.

It seems blindingly obvious to say that only a mother knows what is best for her baby, but every new parent needs reassurance. The problem is, this tends to come with an ideological sting in its tail: co-sleeping is natural, co-sleeping is bad for mother and baby; feeding on demand sets up bad habits, feeding on demand is right and natural; babies should be only breast-fed until at least six months, babies should be given solid food as soon as they show interest in it. Each of these points of view has passionate advocates who are convinced it is the only way to raise a happy baby. And, of course, there is money in telling mothers what to do: the baby-book market is at least three hundred years old. The fact that so many of the books are written by men, or childless women, isn't really surprising. Mothers know from experience that there isn't a right or a wrong way to bring up a baby (apart from the obvious caveats about soft pillows and open flames); there is only the way that works for you.

A look at the different childcare theories of the last three centuries makes it clear that you can't separate them from the societies from which they sprung. New Zealand childcare expert Sir Frederick Truby King's iron routines became popular just after the First World War when the nation needed sturdy independent little soldiers who would be ready to fight another one; attachment theorists like Dr Spock took off when a whole generation of women was being urged to stay at home after the Second World War. I dread to think why the routine-based theories of Gina Ford and her ilk are so popular now.

Bringing Up Baby is definitely not another childcare manual. It is intended to be the antidote to all those bossy books that make even the most strong-minded among us feel inadequate – and, dare I say it, to well-meaning family members of a different generation who can have a very similar effect. It should also be a consolation to any woman who is worried that her lack of mothering skills is in some way harming her baby. A quick glance through its pages will show that childcare advice has veered from one extreme to the other over the last three hundred years, yet the human race has miraculously survived. The chances are your baby will do just fine whether you read the baby books or not.

-1-

Nine Months Inside

*It's the most exciting time of your life.
You've found out you're pregnant,
and from the moment you see that
thin blue line you know things will
never be the same again.*

The history of man for the nine months preceding his birth would probably be far more interesting, and contain events of greater moment, than all the three score and ten years that follow it.
SAMUEL TAYLOR COLERIDGE

And, right from the start, you will find that you are the target of a lot of informed, misinformed, and plain weird advice. Your bookshelves will groan with baby books as you try to work out where you will fit on the spectrum of motherhood: earth mother, control freak, executive mum, stay-at-home mum, yummy mummy … ?

Suddenly, your body is no longer your private property. Strangers shout at you in the street: 'Boy or girl?' or 'When's it due?' (my least favourite was 'Any minute now!' at a portly six months pregnant). You will face a plethora of tests, exams (more than you ever had at school) and anxiety-inducing check-ups before the big day when the baby arrives. Oh, and let's not forget the joy of antenatal classes, breastfeeding classes and pregnancy yoga. You're going to be really busy, and you haven't even had the baby yet!

Euphemisms for Pregnancy

In many ways, pregnancy is the most unambiguous condition you can be in. Yet, because of its inevitable association with sex, its existence used to be shrouded in a cloak of verbiage that could rival Harry Potter's Cloak of Invisibility. In the eighteenth century, according to Harriet Blodger in *A Century of Female Days*, women were 'with child', 'in a family' or 'in the encreasing', although 'pregnancy' was occasionally used. In the sixteenth and seventeenth centuries, being in labour was to be 'in travail' or 'in labor', while in the seventeenth to the nineteenth we were 'lying in', 'delivered of' or 'brought to bed'. In the later seventeenth century a child was also 'born', but in the eighteenth and nineteenth centuries the most popular term was 'confined' – as in 'I was confined'.

It's an odd word to use for what should be a joyful event, but perhaps it summed up some mothers' feelings about being forced to stay without visitors in the lying-in room for as long as a month. Still, some of the old phrases are preferable to our modern 'up the duff', 'knocked up', 'one in the oven' and, of course, 'expecting'.

~ THE FIRST TRIMESTER ~

Quest. What is the Reason that when Women with Child long for Fruits, &c. the mark of that which they long for is often Imprinted in some part of the child's Body?
Answ. The Imaginations of pregnant Women, their Humours being extreamly stirr'd and disturb'd, must needs be very strong and lively.
THE OXFORD DICTIONARY OF SUPERSTITIONS

If one thing sums up the modern age it's anxiety over what goes into our bodies. Perhaps the scary knowledge of how much pollution and chemicals there are 'out there' has turned us all into diet obsessives, worrying about our nutrition while simultaneously heating up ready meals in the microwave.

In the eighteenth century, as the quote above shows, there were concerns about a pregnant woman's cravings literally imprinting themselves on the body of her child as birthmarks. But often the modern obsession with what pregnant women eat doesn't seem very different, especially if you are the confused mother-to-be agonising over whether shellfish are safe or not, or whether you should avoid putting on those pregnancy pounds. Sometimes it's easy to conclude that many experts would prefer it if babies were gestated in artificial wombs, Brave New World style, rather than left to unreliable human hosts.

Of course, having the responsibility of being pregnant means you will want to be more careful than you might have been when you only had yourself to look after. You may want to switch to eating mainly organic food (if you can afford it), for example. But do you really have to spend the amount of time and energy dictated by the Best-Odds Daily Dozen diet described in *What to Expect When You're Expecting*, written by Arlene Eisenberg with her two daughters, Heidi E. Murkoff and Sandee E. Hathaway?

~~~~~~

Protein:
Four servings daily

Vitamin C foods:
Two servings daily

Calcium foods:
Four servings daily green leafy and yellow vegetables, and yellow fruits:
Three servings daily, or more

Other fruits and vegetables:
Two servings daily, or more

Whole grains and legumes:
Six to eleven servings a day

Iron-rich foods:
Some daily

High-fat foods:
Four full or eight half-servings, or an equivalent combination, daily

Salty foods:
In moderation

Fluids:
At least eight 8-ounce glasses daily

~~~~~~

It's not that it's such a horrendous diet; it's the measuring of tiny servings (including cooking oil in your daily fat tally) and weekly weighing, and the more-than-slightly sanctimonious tone that would make any woman want to reach straight for the biscuit tin (chocolate Hob Nobs, yes please!). The best advice is to eat healthily and nutritiously, as you would for yourself, but for heaven's sake don't weld yourself to the scales or flip out if you have eaten a piece of chocolate. As Rachel Cusk says in *A Life's Work*:

'Like a bad parent, the literature of pregnancy bristles with threats and the promise of reprisal, with ghoulish hints at the consequences of thoughtless actions … When you raise your fork to your lips, read one book on this subject, look at it and think, Is this the best bite I can give my baby? If the answer is no, put your fork down.'

The emphasis has shifted from 'What to avoid, and what is best for your growing baby' to 'How to create the healthiest, most intelligent, wonderful baby who ever existed'. We live in such a competitive, anxiety-ridden age that we feel we have to maximise our baby's chances of being not just healthy and happy but also smarter than the rest. Relax. You will no doubt encounter the dreaded 'competitive mum' in a year or two when you go to playgroups – but do you actually want to be her before you've even had your baby?

~
Cravings

Cravings, cravings, cravings. The jury is out on these: most medical authorities grudgingly admit their existence – many women experience them very strongly – but are slightly disapproving. This is what Dr Miriam Stoppard has to say in *Conception, Pregnancy and Birth*:

> ### *Odd tastes and cravings*
> *Saliva often reflects the chemical content of the blood and, with rising hormone levels, the taste within your mouth can change, often being described as metallic. This can also make the taste of certain foods different from normal, with some that you may usually enjoy (coffee is a common example) even becoming intolerable. There is no real scientific explanation for cravings, which can occasionally be for very odd things such as coal, but they are thought to be the body's response to deficiency in certain minerals and trace elements. Try to control or distract cravings for inedible substances as well as high-calorie foods that are low in nutritional value. Otherwise, feel free to indulge yourself within reason.*

I like the instruction to 'distract cravings for inedible substances'. Stories of women eating coal and chalk have been around for centuries. In *Hints to Mothers* one late-nineteenth-century pundit, Thomas Bull, tells the cautionary tale of the Woman Who Ate Chalk and Eventually Died ('she became nearly as white as the substance itself') before moving on to the Ginger-bread-maker's Wife:

> *In reference to the longings of pregnant women for extraordinary articles of food, and on the supposed importance of gratifying them, it may be useful to make a few remarks. For ... there is abundant evidence to prove that the indulgence by the mother in luxurious and unwholesome*

articles of diet not only injures her health, but seriously interferes with the growth and vigour of her offspring ... Dr Merriman [the Compendium of Midwifery, p113–] gives the following striking example of the fatal effects of such indulgence on the child:-

A young woman married to a ginger-bread-maker took a fancy, during her first pregnancy, to chew ginger. The quantity of this spice which she thus consumed was estimated at several pounds. She went her full time, and had a favourable labour; but the child was small and meagre, its skin was discoloured and rough, much resembling the furfuraceous desquamation that takes place after scarlatina. The child continued in an ill state of health for several weeks, and then died.

For Thomas Bull, pregnant patients were stubborn, wilful and ignorant types whose only hope of surviving pregnancy intact and with healthy children was to follow his advice to the letter. It's nice to know little has changed! And it's interesting that ginger, now wheeled out as a safe cure for morning sickness, was once viewed as a baddie.

It worked for me

I had lots of cravings. I'd walk to the shop and buy three jars of pickled onions and some cheese. I'd get home and cut the cheese into cubes and eat it with the pickled onions. I also had to have a cream doughnut every day, and a Muslim colleague of mine would actually go to the store and buy me a bacon sandwich when I got too uncomfortable to walk far. *Sarah, mother of Emily (2 years)*

~
Morning Sickness

In the eighteenth century Hester Thrale, a close friend of Dr Samuel Johnson's, who had 12 pregnancies during her marriage to Mr Thrale, described her first marriage as 'holding my head over a Bason Six Months in the Year'.

In 1850, William Ranking, MD, Cantab., had this to say on the subject in *Ranking's Abstracts*:

> **Vomiting during pregnancy.**
> *Dr. Stoltz, of Strasburg, lays down the following rules.*
>
> *The first thing to be done when we have to treat a pregnant woman affected with obstinate vomiting, is to examine carefully whether the affection be the result of simple pregnancy or whether there be any complication. In the latter case, the first indication is to treat the complications. Thus if there be signs of plethora, venesection must be practiced, without any anxiety as to the term to which pregnancy has advanced. We may also have recourse to the application of leeches to the hypogastrium, to the upper part of the thighs, or to the perineum … If there be a feeling of uneasiness in the gastric region, we adopt a mild antiphlogistic treatment, apply some leeches to the epigastrium, give cooling drinks, and administer laxative enemata; a remedy which is by far preferable to evacuant medicines.*

It worked for me

The only thing that stopped me being sick when I was first pregnant was pear drops. I developed a huge craving for them and would walk miles to find old-fashioned sweet shops to buy them by the pound. They did terrible things to my teeth but they were the only things that kept me from spending the first three months with my head in a basin. *Maggie, mother of Otis (9 months)*

Dr Meigs states that in a great number of the cases of obstinate vomiting in pregnancy, the symptom may be suspended by causing the patient to take a cup of hot coffee and dry toast very early in the morning, after which she is to be quiet till her usual time of rising.

'Dr Meigs please!' I imagine Mr Ranking's female readers ('modest matrons and maidens') crying as one.

In *Hints to Mothers* Thomas Bull was pretty knowledgeable about morning sickness and how it comes and goes in the typical pregnant lady:

She awakes refreshed and well, rises from her bed and while dressing, begins to feel qualmish ... at the breakfast table she has no appetite ... After the lapse of three or four hours she begins to feel quite well again, and at dinner time sits down with appetite to her meal.

His suggestions to help morning sickness include a cold compress around the abdomen, a tincture of 'magnesia, fifteen grains; tincture of calumba, one drachm, and distilled peppermint water, one ounce and a half' and camomile tea. Infusion of calumba, a popular remedy back then, is tea made from calumba root, a herbal medicine used for poor digestion. At least Mr Bull's recipes, like those of Dr Miegs, would probably not have harmed the patient.

~
Anxiety and Stress

[Paris, November 1793]
'Sunday Night.
I have just received your letter, and feel as if I could not go to bed tranquilly without saying a few words in reply, merely to tell you that my mind is serene, and my heart affectionate.

Ever since you last saw me inclined to faint, I have felt some gentle twitches, which make me begin to think that I am nourishing a creature who will soon be sensible of my care. This thought has not only produced an overflowing of tenderness to you, but made me very attentive to calm my mind and take exercise, lest I should destroy an object, in whom we are to have a mutual interest, you know. Yesterday – do not smile! – finding that I had hurt myself by lifting precipitately a large log of wood, I sat down in an agony, till I felt those said twitches again.
Are you very busy?'

This letter from Mary Wollstonecraft, mother of Mary Shelley, to her first lover and the father of her first child (he deserted them both, but she went on to marry again) shows that worry during pregnancy is not restricted to the modern age. Nor was fatigue, as Mary's second child, Mary Shelley, writing to her husband the poet Percy Bysshe Shelley, makes clear:

'My love my own one be happy –
I was so dreadfully tired yesterday that I was obliged to take a coach home forgive this extravagance but I am so very weak at present & I have been so agitated through the day that I was not able to stand a moment ~ rest however will set me quite right again and I shall be quite well when I meet you this evening. Will you be at the door of the coffee house at five o'clock as it is disagreeable to go into those places and I shall be there exactly at that time & we will go into St. Pauls where we can sit down.'

It's all very well trying to keep positive and think nice thoughts, but what if you are really worried about something, or feeling stressed? Reaching for the baby manuals for reassurance can send even the toughest woman weeping to her doctor because there seems to be so much that can go wrong. And, of course, worrying is worrying in itself; it's all too easy to believe too much stress will have an impact on our baby.

'Early stress produces neurophysiological deficits that render children excessively impulsive and irritable. Their condition is further aggravated by a chain of linked factors consisting of poor language skills, poor abstract reasoning, inability to concentrate, and lack of interest in reading. In concert, these factors inevitably lead to academic failure and early dropping out of school, which in turn often lead to a life of addiction and crime.'

This is from *Tomorrow's Baby* by Americans T. Verny and P. Weintraub, 'experts' in prenatal parenting. It shows the kind of dodgy logic, pseudoscience and all-embracing precepts foisted upon parents-to-be in the guise of advice. I like the way the problem is escalated from inability to concentrate to 'a life of addiction and crime' with those sneaky little words 'inevitably' and 'often'.

Even in the eighteenth century women worried about stress. Here is Lady Mary Wortley Montagu, aristocrat and ambassador's wife, who brought inoculation against smallpox from Turkey to England, writing to her husband during her first pregnancy:

'DEC 1712 LM TO WORTLEY

I continue indifferently well, and endeavor as much as I can to preserve my selfe from Spleen and Melancholy, not for My own sake — I think that of little importance but in the condition I am, I beleive it may be of very ill consequence; yet passing whole days alone, as I do, I do not allways find it possible, and my constitution will sometimes get the better of my Reason. Humane Nature it selfe, without any Additional misfortunes, furnishes disagreable meditations enough. Life it selfe, to make it supportable, should not be consider'd too near. My reason represents to me in vain the inutillity of Serious Refections. The idle Mind will sometimes fall into Contemplations that serve for nothing but to ruine the Health, destroy good Humour, hasten old Age and wrinkles, and bring on an Habitual Melancholy …

I am insensibly falln into the writeing you a Melancholy letter, after all my resolutions to the Contrary, but I do not enjoyn you to read it. Make no scruple of flinging it into the Fire at the first dull Line. Forgive the ill Effects of my Solitude, and think me (as I am) ever Yours.'

Some experts on stress during pregnancy may conclude that mothers-to-be should avoid all paid work. But not everyone has the luxury of making this choice. For many women a mortgage or family income may hinge on their being able to work. As the American writer Patrick D Wadwha notes:

The unqualified notion that all stress during pregnancy is harmful to a foetus may also prompt a certain degree of anxiety and self-blame in women. Ironically, this reaction may spiral in some women, who may be unable to change their circumstances (because they need to work to support the family, for example) and may lead to more subjective stress as they contemplate their stressful lives.

Irony, indeed. What is the difference between subjective and objective stress, anyway? For a bit of light relief, let's contemplate the advice of an earlier expert in stress avoidance. This is what Dr Spock had to say in 1957 about the impact of a first pregnancy, in *The Common Sense Book of Baby and Child Care*:

> *To some degree, the first pregnancy spells the end of carefree youth — very important to Americans. The maidenly figure goes gradually into eclipse, and with it sprightly grace. Both eclipses are temporary but very real. The woman realizes that after the baby comes there will be distinct limitations of social life and other outside pleasures. No more hopping into the car on the spur of the moment, going anywhere the heart desires and coming home at any old hour. The same budget has to be spread thinner, and her husband's attention, all of which has gone to her at home, will soon be going to two.*

Interestingly, Spock does not address the impact of a first pregnancy on the husband. Perhaps he wasn't expected to have any limitations on 'outside pleasures'?

~ Antenatal Classes

My mother, Jocasta, remembers antenatal classes where explicit birth films caused pregnant women to pass out; and I remember being traumatised by recordings the teacher played of the birth of her own child. However, most classes sensibly don't go in for too much graphic detail, and can be helpful —

even if you forget most of what you are taught by the time you go into labour. Most importantly, they help you make friends with other mothers-to-be.

In 1987 Sheila Kitzinger, the pioneering British author of *Freedom and Choice in Childbirth*, wrote:

> *Whether or not she is working outside the home, every woman with children needs a good informal support network of people who can help out, or substitute for her, when the going gets tough. In the days of large extended families this existed automatically, but many modern women are alone and isolated.*

Kitzinger says this is one of the main reasons why modern mothers-to-be worry about whether they will be able to look after their baby once it is born. Society has become even more atomised since the 1980s and women are less likely to have a support network of family and friends who they can rely on for pregnancy (and childcare, and labour) advice and support. In the 1960s, according to a Netmums survey of 2000 grandmothers, 50 per cent of young families lived near their extended family; in the 2000s it's 38 per cent. So it makes sense to try and cultivate your own 'support network'. Because otherwise, you're stuck with the books – and the Internet!

~

Exercise

You are free to be involved in most sports during pregnancy (until the last trimester), as long as you have been doing that sport regularly before- hand and you pursue it regularly once you are pregnant ... [swimming, yoga, walking and dancing are listed as safe exercises] ...

Practice with Caution

Some sports, such as cycling, skiing, and horseback riding, should not be engaged in once you grow big because your balance is thrown off by the new weight in front. Other activities, including those listed below [jogging, backpacking and sit-ups] should be avoided because they put your body under unnecessary stress that could harm both you and your baby.

This is Miriam Stoppard's advice on exercising during pregnancy, but some of the more laid-back among you will be surprised to find that women are expected to do more when they are pregnant than go to work, try to keep up with the housework and spend the rest of the time sleeping on the sofa. Yet even in the eighteenth century doctors worried that (upper-class) pregnant women were spending too much time lying around and should be being more active. Queen Victoria, on the other hand, expressed disapproval that flighty pregnant mums were to be seen at balls wearing flimsy garments. You can't win!

Modern manuals advise avoiding high-impact exercise during the whole pregnancy, and lying on your back after the first trimester (to avoid putting pressure on the vena cava), but most sports and exercises are approached in a breezy, can-do manner. This is in sharp contrast to earlier manuals, such as *Feeding and Care of Baby* by the New Zealand health reformer, Sir Frederick Truby King, an eccentric mental-hospital director and childcare expert (who became interested in child welfare and nutrition after health concerns over his adopted baby daughter), which suggested little beyond a few gentle exercises (as shown in the photographs overleaf).

Meanwhile, back in the Victorian era, Thomas Bull had more hints for mothers:

> *The error still prevails to some extent, that exercise at the commencement of pregnancy is prejudicial, and should be refrained from almost entirely; but that at the conclusion of gestation its employment is beneficial ...*

Fig. 3. Physical Exercises.

> *That women, as a general rule, should be encouraged to live more indolently (exercise being thought improper unless towards the conclusion of pregnancy, when it is supposed to procure a more favourable delivery), is an error exceedingly injurious. The fact is, a directly contrary method of proceeding is the most eligible and proper – exercise in the early months, with a gradual approach to a state of repose as the period of confinement approaches.*
>
> *During the first six or seven months frequent and gentle exercise in the open air, and domestic occupation, which requires moderate exertion, are very desirable ... Crowded assemblies, however, of all kinds, public spectacles, and large parties – in short everything calculated to rouse strong feelings, to depress the mind, or excite the passions – ought to be sedulously avoided.*

So housework and gentle walks were OK, but parties were out. I suppose the ladies Queen Victoria disapproved of weren't reading Bull's *Hints to Mothers* with enough attention.

Historical research carried out in 2000 by the charity Tommy's Campaign (which works to prevent miscarriage, stillbirth and premature birth) found that in 1900 mothers-to-be were advised to avoid 'exciting books, breath-taking pictures or family quarrels', and not to ride motorcycles or small cars over bumpy roads. Women in the nineteenth century were considered 'temperamentally unsound' if they exercised or rode a bicycle. But more and more is expected of us these days – in 1987 Sheila Kitzinger solemnly warned readers against attempting scuba diving while pregnant (was anyone considering it?).

What Not to Watch When You're Pregnant

Rosemary's Baby: Demonic possession of foetus; need I say more?

Gladiator: The scene where Russell Crowe's son is crucified made my baby adopt a breech position and stay there.

Planet Earth and other wildlife programmes: They always feature a baby elephant/polar bear/giraffe that gets separated from the herd.

Bambi and/or *The Lion King*: Guaranteed to raise a tear at any time but fatal when you're pregnant.

'*The ancient Egyptians had a method for testing both pregnancy and sex at the same time. The woman sprinkled her urine on a few grains of barley and emmer (a kind of wheat). If both sprouted, the test was positive for pregnancy; if the barley did, it was a boy; and if the emmer, then it was a girl. The method was still being used in nineteenth-century Germany and when tested under laboratory conditions in the 1960s, was found to be 70 per cent accurate for confirming pregnancy, although totally unreliable for predicting gender.*'

ROGER GOSDEN

~ THE SECOND TRIMESTER ~

This is the period when you start to feel better and are less affected by the pregnancy. Even though you are bigger, you should be less tired and hopefully start to experience that famous pregnant lady 'glow'.

~
Boy or Girl?

Until science discovered the workings of the X and Y chromosomes, there was confusion over how the sex of a child was determined during conception (Hippocrates, the Greek physician, believed the right testicle produced sons, and that if a daughter was wanted the man should 'tie off the right testicle as much as he can bear'). Even Darwin, the granddaddy of evolutionary theory, had funny ideas about how babies were produced.

According to *A Cultural History of Pregnancy* by Clare Hanson, Darwin objected to the concept of 'maternal impressions' – the widespread superstition that something that scared a pregnant woman would affect the baby. For example, if she was startled by a dog putting its paws on her belly she would give birth to a child with deformed hands; or if she craved a certain fruit it would produce a mark on the baby's body. Instead, his *Zoonomia* suggested it was 'paternal impressions', and what was in the father's mind at the moment of conception, that determined the child's appearance and even its sex. This involved a lot of convoluted explanation as to why the father was thinking of a male at the time of conceiving a boy …

Mystery reigned while a woman was pregnant, and the only way to try to tell whether the baby would be a boy or a girl was to resort to folklore and superstition, as described in *Designer Babies* by Roger Gosden (see opposite).

It's interesting that so many mothers-to-be who choose not to know the sex of their baby by the reliable modern method of ultrasound nonetheless try out the pendulum and other guesswork methods. The Chinese Fertility Calendar is also popular in the United States, as is putting urine in a bottle with some disinfectant (!).

Music in the Womb

There are many new semi-scientific theories about pregnancy, such as the one that you can kick-start your baby's development by listening to classical music, or even language tapes. There are valid reasons for believing that unborn babies are influenced by music, but the jury is out on whether this affects their learning ability or how they develop. Sceptics claim much of the research presupposes that there is somehow something wrong with the way a baby normally develops before birth and assumes that artificial interventions are necessary to 'help' it. Some, such as shining bright lights on the womb, they say might even be harmful. The following is from an article in *Psychology Today*:

Parents-to-be who want to further their unborn child's mental development should start by assuring that the antenatal environment is well nourished, low-stress, drug-free. Various authors and 'experts' also have suggested poking the fetus at regular intervals, speaking to it through a paper tube or 'pregaphone', piping in classical music, even flashing lights at the mother's abdomen. Does such stimulation work? More importantly: Is it safe? Some who use these methods swear their children are smarter, more verbally and musically inclined, more physically coordinated and socially adept than average. Scientists, however, are sceptical ... (SEPTEMBER/OCTOBER 1998)

Professor Peter Hepper of Queen's University, Belfast, says babies do acquire specific likings in the womb. According to his study, published in *The Psychologist* magazine, newborns prefer their mother's voice, enjoy food flavours they were exposed to through amniotic fluid and have a preference for music they heard before they were born. However, he told me that there is no guarantee that hearing music will improve their development:

> *There is no evidence, as far as I am aware, to suggest that the fetus improves its development by listening to music nor that it stands a greater chance of becoming a musician. However there is probably an indirect effect that if the music relaxes the mother then this reduces her stress and the baby's development may be enhanced.*

There seems to be a general consensus that babies prefer soft classical music to loud rock – although they like something with rhythm! If just playing Mozart to your baby doesn't seem enough, you could always try turning yourself into a 'prenatal classroom' like the pregnant lady described in *Magic Trees of the Mind* who followed R. Van de Carr and M. Lehrer's prenatal exercises for a bright baby:

> *The lesson went on to introduce different kinds of contact – patting, rubbing, squeezing, shaking, stroking, tapping – and the accompanying verbs, delivered via paper megaphone. Jeannine [the mother] would stand up, sit down, sway, or rock and say the appropriate verbs. She would drink hot and cold liquids and label the sensation for Lisel [the fetus]. Tony [the father] would turn on a radio speaker ('Music!') or a vacuum cleaner ('Noise!'), or shine a flashlight on and off ('Light!' 'Dark!' 'Light!' 'Dark!'). Every ten minute session, morning and evening, would begin with the 'Hi Baby!' megaphone greeting and end with a few minutes of classical music piped in through headphones.*

It worked for me

Adelaide, who has a background in working with disabilities, had Milly at 37. During her pregnancy she played a CD, entitled 'Music for the Unborn Child', to her and says it helped to calm Millie in the first month after a traumatic birth by Caesarean section. 'Milly is a very bright baby for her age and we feel it played a good part in her development.' *Adelaide, mother of Milly (10 months)*

~ THE THIRD TRIMESTER ~

~ Old Wives' Tales

Bad luck will befall those parents who are expecting a baby, if they make any preparations for its arrival.
If an expectant mother has her picture taken, it will cause bad luck.
If you stoop under a clothes line every time you go out, while pregnant, the baby's navel could be tied around his neck.
SUPERSTITIONS: 10,000 YOU REALLY NEED

The number of old wives' tales is bewildering and, oddly, despite our modern knowledge and understanding of science, it is almost impossible not to take some of them on board. Most cultures have traditions surrounding pregnancy, childbirth and labour, many of which have been handed down for centuries. Pregnancy amulets, for example, were worn to protect the wearer and her baby from evil influences, and I'm sure a lot of modern women have a 'lucky charm' they carried while they were pregnant.

Many superstitions like the ones above are to do with keeping the baby from coming to harm. Even before we knew as much as we do now about how babies develop and the potential risks, women saw pregnancy as an anxious time and the advice they were given reflects this – and still endures today. I was told several times that I shouldn't stretch my hands above my head in case the cord went round the baby's neck, and several people gave me the benefit of their advice as to whether my pregnancy shape indicated a boy or a girl (girls produce a neat bump and boys are more spread out, apparently).

Superstitions about preparing for the baby are common in several cultures. For example, in the United States some mothers-to-be don't have baby showers or kit out a nursery until the last minute, to avoid bad luck. And our own dear Queen didn't have a pram delivered to the palace until after the Prince of Wales was born.

An ancient superstition, and one that most of us probably know, is that pregnant women should not look at certain things as this may affect the baby; for example, if a mother-to-be looks at a fire she will have a red-headed child. Even though we are told this is nonsense, many women are still influenced by this idea; for example, they may avoid violent or disturbing films on television.

In *Freedom and Choice in Childbirth*, Sheila Kitzinger describes this as, in fact, a type of feminine wisdom that occurs with pregnancy. Women start to see themselves as part of the world and less as individuals:

Many women say they respond with strong emotions to suffering, whether of human beings or animals. Tears come quickly, and television programmes which extol violence or vividly depict the consequences of war, and press photographs of starving children with their swollen bellies and stick-like limbs, prove unbearably distressing. It is as if approaching motherhood sensitises you to the needs not only of your own child, but of all the world's children … The world is in short supply of these qualities of nurturing. We often clamp down on such emotions because the exposed nerve causes too much pain.

In the past, experts believed that 'wandering wombs' were the reason why women were more prone to express emotion. We now know it's hormones (and emotional intelligence!), but women's feelings during pregnancy have always been under close scrutiny:

> *The whole habit of the body may be disturbed by a certain state of the uterus, and yet no individual part be peculiarly affected ... In consequence also of this general and perpetual irritation, the temper of pregnant women is sometimes rendered less gentle and patient than is consistent with their usual character.*

This comes from *An Introduction to the Practice of Midwifery* by Thomas Denman, who was a 'man-midwife' in the eighteenth century, when men started taking over and became known as *accoucheurs*. Interestingly, also in the eighteenth century, in her *Advice to the Female Sex in General* Martha Mears, one of the few female midwives to publish a book (she was also a mother), argued strongly against the idea that women were badly affected by pregnancy:

> *The state of pregnancy has too generally been considered as a state of indisposition or disease; this is a fatal error and the source of almost all of the evils to which women in childbearing are liable.*

Sex During Pregnancy

> *Much has been written, and may be found in the innumerable books on the sex-problems, as to whether a man and woman should or should not have relations while the wife is bearing an unborn child ... we cannot but think that the safe side of this debatable question must be in the complete continence of the woman for at least six months before the birth of the child.*

[To demand complete continence for at least six months before the child is born is entirely too severe a requirement. As a woman should for several reasons wait six weeks or two months after the birth of the child before resuming sex relations, it follows that with each pregnancy the husband would have to be abstinent for a period of about eight months. Such complete abstinence would be for some husbands difficult, for some unbearable. For some it might result in very unpleasant complications.]

... While the wife feels that she cannot allow her husband to enter the portals of her body when it has become the sacred temple of a developing life, she should also consider the perpetual strain which nature imposes upon him; and the tender and loving wife will readily find some means of giving him that physical relief which his nature needs.

I find this extract from *Married Love*, published in 1918, particularly fascinating because of the way the (male) editor interrupts the wonderful Marie Stopes to plead for the conjugal rights of husbands. The emphasis is clearly on the man's state of mind; the woman's libido is not an issue.

Modern manuals like Miriam Stoppard's *Conception, Pregnancy and Birth* err in the other direction, suggesting we will feel like randy love-goddesses right up until our first contractions.

Unless there are medical reasons for abstaining, sexual intercourse is safe and permissible in pregnancy. Moreover, every pregnant woman has the potential to enjoy sex – perhaps more than she ever has before ... when a pregnant woman has sex, she may find it far more exciting and satisfying than it was before she conceived. In fact, a woman will sometimes achieve orgasm or multiple orgasms for the first time when she is pregnant ...

The knowledge that prostaglandin from semen can ripen the cervix means that women who are overdue are exhorted to have sex as well as eat curry (not at the same time, obviously) to speed things up. The general medical advice is that sex is fine up to the due date, as long as it is not unusually athletic and doesn't involve sex toys. Generally, though, it must make more sense to do what you feel like, and if that involves more sleep and less sex by the third trimester, that's fine, and probably the best rehearsal you could have for parenthood.

Preparing the Nursery

Preparing a nursery for the baby looms large in first-time mothers' minds, as Gina Ford says in her no-nonsense way in *The New Contented Little Baby Book*:

> *When one talks of preparing for the birth, the first things that spring to mind are antenatal care and decorating the nursery. Both are important in their own ways. Antenatal care is of the utmost importance for a healthy pregnancy and essential to prepare you for the birth, and decorating the nursery for the new arrival is fun.*

Some women might question whether decorating the nursery is all that much fun after reading the daunting list of requirements set out in most manuals. In Gina Ford's book, for example, essentials such as cot, cot sheets and blankets, changing station, changing mat and chair are followed by blackout curtains and a fitted carpet. There is a set of requirements for clothes, then there is the pram, car seat, baby monitor, baby sling and (possibly) a playpen.

Then there is breastfeeding paraphernalia if you're planning to breastfeed, or bottle sterilisation kits if you're not … The list can seem impossibly long, although it is heartening to compare modern requirements with old ones. Here are the clothes Truby King recommends for baby's first year:

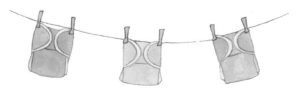

Woollens	2 shawls	next to the skin)
3 knitted singlets	4 flannel triangles	4 petticoats
3 nightgowns	2 pairs fingerless gloves	4 frocks
3 petticoats	Woollen caps, or bonnets	6 bibs
3 jackets	**Cottons**	3 doz. Napkins
4 pairs pilchers	3 cellular cotton shirts,	(27 ins. Square)
6 pairs of bootees	long sleeved (to be worn	3 cotton binders

The Mothercraft Manual by Mabel Liddiard, first published in 1923, adds to this list a dozen nappies, a dozen handkerchiefs 'for baby's own use' and the comment:

> *There is something sad about the woman who is content to buy the outfit ready made. Surely there is a lack of the true mother spirit, for the making of the little garments brings a joy that is all its own. Everything should be practically ready by the seventh month [of pregnancy, that is!].*

It worked for me

Sophie was baffled by the insistence in some books on buying muslin, or Harrington Squares, until she had her first baby. They are useful for preventing a baby being sick on your clothes (drape one over your shoulder when you pick the baby up) and double as comfort cloths. *Sophie, mother of Lily (6 months)*

All this reminds me of the fantastic sketch in *Absolutely Fabulous* where Edwina's interior-designer friend has just had a baby and arrives with a truck-load of kit, horrifying Edwina, whose house has just had a minimalist makeover in her guest's honour. Eventually Edwina offers the husband 'physical relief', knowing the baby intercom is switched on and his wife is listening, just to get rid of them … Here are some sobering statistics, from an American Express survey, on the budget needed for the basic baby kit:

~~~~~~

Average costs of a baby: before birth and during the first year

Pregnancy clothes £132

Pregnancy toiletries £45

Nursery furniture/decorations £150

Cot £160

Bedding £100

Pram £233

Car seat £79

Baby carrier £25

Changing mat £6

Baby bath £18

Baby monitor £30

Baby skincare products £120

Baby wipes £240

Steriliser £20

Formula milk (average £50
   per month) £600

Bottles £20

Baby food £360

High chair £50

Clothes (first year total) £280

Disposable nappies
   (first year total) £500

Safety gates £40

Toys/accessories £142

Baby bouncer £30

Total for first year £3380

~~~~~~

~

Giving Birth

Things have improved a great deal since the bad old days quoted in Sheila Kitzinger's *Freedom and Choice in Childbirth*:

> *Take this account of birth written from a woman's point of view in the thirties – and intended to be reassuring to the expectant mother. It starts by telling her: 'The thing to have firmly fixed in your mind ... is that you are going to be a good girl', and warns her that the way to get the best out of doctors and nurses is to do what she is told. Then there is a description of what she can expect in labour:*
>   *'Time passes but she is not aware of it as she lies in 'a merciful stupor,*

not knowing, not caring ... conscious, but foggy ... in pain, but it doesn't seem real.' Something jolts her out of peaceful quiescence. She is put on a stretcher and carried to another room but doesn't really know what is happening to her – because everything is completely confused, 'like a nightmare'. All she feels is pain. 'Then a rubber ring is fitted over your face ... you gulp in great breaths. Pinpricks of light and a grinding noise that goes round in a spiral zooms through your head.' ... After a time she opens her eyes to see that there is a nurse in the room. She starts to remember that there was something about a baby – and asks, 'When am I going to have the baby?' and a nurse announces, 'You have a fine son born three hours ago.'

You can sense the indignation in Sheila Kitzinger's tone (she is a campaigner who has made a great difference to British obstetric practices) as she describes the standard medicalised experience for women only fifty years before she wrote her book.

Yet in 1853 Queen Victoria was thrilled to have been unconscious during the birth of her seventh child, Prince Leopold. She later wrote in her journal, 'Dr Snow gave that blessed chloroform and the effect was soothing, quieting and delightful beyond measure.' For once, she'd found an exception to 'nasty doctors'! Her example was followed gratefully by many women.

In the eighteenth and nineteenth centuries most women gave birth at home, and before doctors took over the process some of them were able to take childbirth very much in their stride. An example is Mrs Guest, in *A Century of Female Days* by Harriet Blodger, whose relaxed approach to her tenth confinement in August 1847 makes one gasp:

I had rather suspected I might soon be confined, but I went to sleep and forgot it. In the morning when I woke I became pretty sure the event was not far distant. I merely told Merthyr I would breakfast upstairs, which I did. I suffered scarcely at all, and at half past 10 gave birth to another little girl, our 5th daughter and 10th child ... I sent for Merthyr, who did not even know I was indisposed, and showed him our new treasure.

As far back as the seventeenth century, the anonymous author of *Age Rectified* (a handbook for women) suggested that the older woman could play a useful part in society as a midwife or nurse, and shows an understanding of how important it was to have female support during labour and pregnancy:

A teeming [ie breeding] Woman can have not better Incouragement or Assistance than from such an experience'd Friend in time of need. And young Children can hardly be brought up without the Advice and Directions of those, who have before had the like Care. These tender Fibres are soon disorder'd thro Inadvertency: numerous Ailments attend them, which an unwary Eye serves not till a worse consequence follows, and a common remedy might at first have rectified. Even celebrated Nurses will often overlook many Symptoms, Which an affectionate By-Stander may discover, and Find a sutable remedy for, from their own Experience.

Hester Thrale's *Children's Book* gives a great deal of information about what pregnancy and childbirth were like for this talented literary friend of Dr Johnson in the eighteenth century. Of her second pregnancy she wrote, 'I never had a Day's Health during the whole Gestation – the Labour was however particularly short & easy.' Once she was sitting with Dr Johnson when 'I felt sudden & violent pains come on; I hasted to bed' – and gave birth within two hours. Some of her labours were easy, others, when the baby was overdue, were difficult (she once referred to herself as being like a convict: 'twelve confinements with hard labour'). Once she wrote about a baby only that she was 'large & likely to live'; after another, 'The Labour was rough & tight, but no Boy nor no Death ensued'; after another, 'the Lying In is delightful'!

It worked for me

The most useful thing I bought was a breastfeeding pillow. I used it to help me sleep at night when I was pregnant. It was great for when I was breastfeeding Max and now he is weaned he sometimes sits propped up against it. *Chloe, mother of Max (1 year)*

~

The Pregnancy Suitcase

This list (edited down) from Miriam Stoppard's *Conception, Pregnancy and Birth* includes clothes and personal effects for yourself, clothes and nappies for the baby and 'comfort aids' during labour:

~~~~~~

For yourself

Two or three maternity
  bras and front-opening
  cotton nightdresses
Breast pads
Bathrobe and slippers
Underpants
Sanitary towels
Hairbrush and shampoo
Towels and washcloths
Small mirror
Make-up
Lotion
Tissues
Birth plan

For your baby

Nappies
Baby clothes
Nightshirt
Hat
Blanket
Carrier/car seat

Comfort aids during labour

Food and drink (for your
  partner during labour,
  and you afterwards)
Spinal roll or tennis ball
Massage oil or powder
Hot-water bottle
Magazines, board games,
  etc.
Container of ice [to suck]
Small natural sponge [ditto]

Washcloth and hand-held
  fan
Leg warmers or thick socks
Hairpins, barrettes or hair-
  band
Lip salve
Toothbrush and tooth-
  paste
Box of tissues or baby wipes
Cologne
A pack of freshening wipes
  for face and hands
Change of
  clothing (for
  your partner)
Camera and film,
  or video camera,
  if permitted
Coins and phone card
  with numbers of family
  and friends

~~~~~~

As you can see, it's possible to bring everything but the kitchen sink to the delivery room, and equally possible that you will forget to use all of it once you are in labour, so I recommend taking these lists with a pinch of salt, apart from the baby's car seat, which is mandatory (top tip: practise installing it in your car *before* you go into labour so you are not waiting outside the hospital while your partner fiddles with it!).

~

The Expectant Father

The following extract is from 'The Making of a Modern Dad', an article in *Psychology Today*:

It takes a lot more than testosterone to make a father out of a man ... Two Canadian studies suggest that there is much more to masculinity ... While testosterone is certainly important in driving men to conceive a child, it takes an array of other hormones to turn men into fathers. And among the best fathers, it turns out, testosterone levels actually drop significantly after the birth of a child. If manhood includes fatherhood, which it does for a majority of men, then testosterone is hardly the ultimate measure of masculinity.

In fact, the second of the two studies, which was recently published in the Mayo Clinic Proceedings, suggests that fathers have higher levels of estrogen – the well-known female sex hormone – than other men. The research shows that men go through significant hormonal changes alongside their pregnant partners – changes most likely initiated by their partner's pregnancy and ones that even cause some men to experience pregnancy-like symptoms such as nausea and weight gain. It seems increasingly clear that just as nature prepares women to be committed moms, it prepares men to be devoted dads.

(MARCH/APRIL 2002)

The phenomenon of Couvade Syndrome, when men suffer the same 'symptoms' as their pregnant partners (nausea and getting fat, that is – not having a baby!) has been around for a long time but has only recently gained scientific recognition. It seems extraordinary, but it goes to show how intense the experience of pregnancy is even for the woman's partner.

So don't forget: not only is your partner on the same kind of emotional rollercoaster as you, he may even be experiencing some of the same effects. An NOP poll for *Bella* magazine found that up to 10 per cent of new dads in London and 4 per cent nationwide suffered from depression following the birth of their baby. Symptoms included tiredness, loss of libido and irritability.

Traditionally, expectant fathers were kept out of labour and delivery rooms and were not expected to do more than wait outside for the glad tidings. This was also true of the prehospital era of home deliveries: birth was seen as a female-only event and men were expected to be elsewhere, unless they were surgeons or (later) male-midwives and doctors. It was only in the 1960s, when women found themselves alone and frightened in hospital delivery rooms, that the tide began to turn and the medical profession started to think it was a good idea to let the fathers in.

Nowadays 90 per cent of fathers in the United Kingdom have been there at the birth. There is a move against this trend, however. In 2000, Dr Michael Odent, who invented the birthing pool, said he thought men were not always the best birthing partners. He suggested that overanxious fathers might be responsible for an upsurge in Caesarean sections because they cannot stand seeing their partners in pain. 'The baby's father – a man – is not always the best possible person to help his wife to feel secure.'

Mary Newburn, head of policy research at the National Childbirth Trust, agreed with him to some extent: 'Many couples will decide that it is right for the father to be there through labour and see his child being born, but that is not right for everybody.'

In the 1950s, in the days before dads were allowed to be present at births, Dr Spock suggested that the best place for the father-to-be was probably the bar – not an idea modern parents would be very keen on.

The father is apt to feel particularly left out during the hospital period with his first baby. He helps to get his wife safely to the hospital, where there are dozens of people to take care of her. Then he's really alone, with nothing to do outside working hours. He can sit in the waiting room with some old magazines and worry about how the labor is going, or he can go to his unbelievably lonely home. It's no wonder that a man may take this occasion to drink in company at a bar ... the hospital doesn't make him feel like the head of the family; he's just another visitor who's tolerated at certain hours ...

The father is apt to get the mistaken idea that he's unimportant.

He's apt to feel less important than usual and therefore let down.

Of course, the experience of birth is most traumatic for the baby. I love the poem by Thom Gunn on the following page about the horror of being born:

Baby Song

From the private ease of Mother's womb
I fall into the lighted room.

Why don't they simply put me back
Where it is warm and wet and black?

But one thing follows on another.
Things were different inside Mother.

Padded and jolly I would ride
The perfect comfort of her inside.

They tuck me in a rustling bed
I lie there, raging, small and red.

I may sleep soon, I may forget,
But I won't forget that I regret.

A rain of blood poured round her womb.
But all time roars outside this room.

THOM GUNN

-2-

And Now The Fun Begins

*In my experience most mothers aren't
in any condition to really supervise the first
few moments of their baby's life, but this hasn't
stopped the experts bombarding them with
advice about how to welcome a newborn
into the world.*

'Once your baby is delivered, all of the attention will be given to her, not to you, and rightly so … If her breathing is normal, there's no reason why you should not hold her immediately. If there's a danger of her being cold, you can be covered with a towel or blanket. Your gentle stroking movements and the sound of your heartbeat and voice will reassure your baby. Her eyes will almost certainly fasten on your face, and she may scrabble as if trying to swim towards you … As you hold her you will experience the glow of motherhood – a mixture of love, pride, awe, and wonder, mixed with the all-encompassing tiredness that comes with a hard job well done … It's a good idea to put the baby to the breast immediately because it stimulates the delivery of the placenta, even if your baby isn't hungry at first.'

This description of the first few moments after the birth of a twenty-first-century baby is from Dr Miriam Stoppard's *Conception, Pregnancy and Birth*. There are assumptions, such as the one that you will bond instantly to your baby and that you will certainly want to breastfeed, which don't always echo every mother's experiences, but it's a warm and friendly description of a newborn's introduction to the planet. Here's an account, from Christina Hardyment's *Perfect Parents*, of an eighteenth-century baby's first minutes and days of life in England, which makes you wonder how, having survived the dangerous birth process, any infants made it past day three at all:

> *At the beginning of the eighteenth century, the typical baby was helped into the world by a self taught midwife, licked with the 'basting tongue', or scoured with salt to remove the 'slippery glue' from its skin, and tightly swaddled onto a board. Its head was wrapped in 'compresses three, four, or five times doubled', pinned to a cap, and further braced by a tight neck stay ... While the half-strangled baby hung from a nail, its minder could get on with other tasks ... The baby would not be put to the breast until the mother's milk was seen to come in, perhaps on the second or third day. Meanwhile, purges were applied 'to cleanse the child of its long-hoarded Excrement'. Oil of almond, syrup of roses and chicory with rhubarb were accepted recipes.*

Wine was also an accepted substitute food – for baby rather than mother!

During the eighteenth and nineteenth centuries babies were typically born at home in the 'lying-in room', although a few lying-in hospitals were being built by the mid-1850s. By the early twentieth century hospitals were increasingly popular; in the 1909 domestic manual *The Book of the Home*, new mothers are urged to have all the medical intervention possible:

> *The woman who cannot afford a doctor is to be pitied. Every effort and self-denial should be employed to secure such attendance, because it is not a true economy to save in this matter by having a midwife.*

But by the 1960s, when most women had their babies in hospital, the tide began to turn back towards the desirability of home births. Having a baby in hospital, where it was whisked off to the nursery, meant many mothers found it difficult to establish breastfeeding.

In 1975, in *The Continuum Concept*, Jean Liedloff, an eccentric WASP ex-model and writer who lived with and studied a remote Amazonian tribe, described the typical maternity-ward experience in the United States with great indignation:

> *The newborn infant with his skin crying out for the ancient touch of smooth, warmth-radiating, living flesh, is wrapped in dry, lifeless cloth. He is put in a box where he is left, no matter how he weeps, in a limbo which is utterly motionless (for the first time in all his body's experience, during the eons of its evolution or during its eternity of bliss in the womb). The only sounds he can hear are the wails of other victims of the same ineffable agony … a timeless lifetime later, he falls asleep exhausted … [There follows a description of the baby's loneliness as he yearns for his mother's touch, cries and wets himself. His nappy is changed on schedule, rather than because he is wet. Finally he is taken to his mother for a feed.] Someone comes and lifts him deliciously through the air. He is in life. He is carried a bit too gingerly for his taste, but there is motion. Then he is in his place … The taste and texture of the breast are there, the warm milk is flowing into his eager mouth, there is a heartbeat with all its comforting, there is movement perceptible to his dim vision … [The baby is returned to his cot.] When he awakes he is in hell.*

It was a change in psychological opinion in the 1970s that emphasised how important mothers were to newborn infants and gave them a chance to get close to their babies soon after birth. Theories of attachment, based on a study of rhesus monkeys by John Bowlby, had shown that maternal contact was as important to babies as food. Baby monkeys showed a preference for a soft, huggable cotton 'mother' as opposed to a wire 'mother', even when the wire one was equipped with feeding teats and the cotton one was not. Again, it took a study to show the medical profession what had always been obvious to mothers.

Here's a description from *John Bowlby and Attachment Theory* of a family photograph that shows Bowlby, the father of attachment parenting, as a four-year-old:

> *A family photograph, taken just before the First World War, shows Lady Bowlby surrounded by her six children. Her husband, Sir Anthony, the King's surgeon, is not there – he is, as usual, at work. She is flanked by her two favourite sons, John and Tony, aged about four and five … on her lap sits the baby Evelyn. The two older girls … stand dutifully and demurely to one side. Finally there is two-year-old Jim, the weak member of the family, dubbed a 'late developer', lacking the physical and intellectual vigour of his brothers and sisters. A hand appears around his waist, partly propping him up. But whose hand can it be? Is it his mother's? No, hers are firmly around the baby – a rare moment of physical closeness, as it turned out. Can it be one of his older sisters? No their hands are politely by their sides. It is in fact the hand of an invisible nurse, crouching behind the* tableau vivant, *the tiny and perfectionist 'Nanna Friend' who provided the child care …*

It is easy to see how the 'hands off', physically remote upbringing experienced by Bowlby (and fairly typical of his generation and background) led to his interest in children's attachment to their mothers and how it causes grief when the attachment is broken (maternal deprivation).

Bonding with Your Baby

Here is an extract from what is described as 'a very candid conversation' with Jean Liedloff, published in *Touch The Future* magazine:

When the baby is first born things are stuck up its nose and down its throat to clear them. Then it's weighed and measured, which isn't doing it any good at this very sensitive moment. For what, the Bureau of Statistics?

What the baby needs is to be in its mother's arms, and the mother even more so needs to have the baby in her arms to share this beautiful moment of falling in love, which is exquisitely choreographed by hormones.

If you were exhausted after giving birth you could say, 'Oh well forget it. Just drop that little stranger in the river. Or just leave it there for a minute. I'll be back later,' at which time the wolves might have gobbled it up.

It's very important to have this great moment of falling in love, known as bonding. It's built in because it has to be for our survival. It has to have been there for us to have become the successful species we are, successful meaning that we survived.

(FALL 1998)

Bonding is a concept adopted from the work of two Australian researchers, Marshall Klaus and John Kennel. Their studies of herd animals (yes, really) and Guatemalan peasant women led them to suggest, in 1976, that it happens between mother and baby in an extremely short space of time, shortly after birth, and involves close physical contact. Failure to bond could lead to emotional distance between them, and psychological damage to the child in later life.

Jean Liedloff also saw bonding after birth as important, as it fits into her Continuum theory (that human nature needs to be in tune with its ancient needs rather than the demands of modern life). As she implies above, if you don't bond with your baby immediately, you may have left it vulnerable to predators.

Bonding was adopted as gospel by maternity wards and bodies like the National Childbirth Trust, and scepticism about the concept only began to appear in the late 1980s when Penelope Leach, for example, wrote in *Baby and Child* in 1988 that bonding 'is not an exhortation to parents, but to delivery room staff, who should not get between the post-natal three-some for a bustle of routine care until there has been the time and opportunity for them all to greet one another.'

In other words, bonding was not a medical necessity but an important part of adjusting to becoming a parent. Many parents who were not able to have physical contact with their children straight away for medical reasons, felt very guilty about missing out on the bonding period. Nowadays, women are given the opportunity to hold their babies directly after birth, but are no longer led to believe that not doing so will cause them lasting psychological harm.

Too Posh to Bond

The royal family has never been very good at the warm, fuzzy maternal stuff. Here is Queen Victoria debunking the wonder of childbirth in a letter to Vicky, the eldest of her nine children – it is one of a number she wrote to the Princess Royal, collected under the title *Dearest Child*.

'What you say of the pride of giving life to an immortal soul is very fine, dear, but I own I cannot enter into that; I think much more of our being like a cow or a dog at such moments.'

Despite having nine children, Queen Victoria didn't appear to enjoy motherhood. Attachment gurus would argue that this was because she hardly ever saw the little darlings as they were looked after 24/7 by a battalion of nursemaids. All the royal children had wet nurses, which was standard upper-class practice at the time.

Queen Victoria admitted openly in her letters that she didn't really like babies much, preferred the children she spent the least time with, and resented the fact that having babies interfered with her relationship with Prince Albert and her social life.

'I have no adoration for very little babies … ' she writes. 'An ugly baby is a very nasty object – and the prettiest is frightful when undressed … ' Poor Leopold, one of her youngest children (born in 1853), was particularly unpopular:

> *I hope, dear, he [Vicky's young son] won't be like [Leopold] the ugliest and least pleasing of the whole family.*

She tells Vicky that, like Leopold, she wasn't one of her favourite children. The reason? Queen Victoria spent too much time with her and Bertie (the Prince of Wales):

> *I never cared for you near as much as you seem to about the baby; I care much more for the younger ones (poor Leopold perhaps excepted) … We used to constantly see you and Bertie in bed and bathed – and we only see the younger ones [being bathed and in bed] – once in three months perhaps.*

It worked for me

My husband was going on an all-expenses trip to the Far East just a week after my second child was due. I was determined to go with him so I booked a 24-hour baby nurse. My daughter was born two days before we had to leave, so I literally came home from the hospital, gave the baby to the nurse and went straight to the airport. I had a fabulous time with my husband and was thrilled to be reunited with my daughter when I got back. Obviously the breastfeeding fundamentalists were horrified by my behaviour, but I think a happy mother makes for a happy baby. *Anna, mother of four*

The children's sumptuous nursery, decorated and furnished as it would have been in their day, can still be seen in the royal family's holiday home, Osborne House on the Isle of Wight. Judging from her letters, Queen Victoria spent very little time here when her children were small.

Breast Wasn't Always Best

In 1860 Queen Victoria, the ultimate Victorian mother, wrote this to her daughter Vicky about childbirth and nursing:

Oh! if those selfish men – who are the cause of all one's misery – only knew what their poor slaves go through! What suffering – what humiliation to the delicate feelings of a poor woman, above all a young one – especially with those nasty doctors … Especially the horrors about that peculiarly indelicate nursing (which is far worse than all the other parts).

Queen Victoria loathed 'nursing' so much that she got distinctly irritated with two of her daughters when they insisted on breastfeeding their children despite her instructions to the contrary. Her distaste was to be echoed throughout the late nineteenth century and the first half of the twentieth as breastfeeding became distinctly unfashionable. This is what Mrs Panton has to say in *The Way They Should Go*, a popular manual for a model young couple, written in the late nineteenth century:

> *Let no mother condemn herself to be a common or ordinary 'cow' unless she has a real desire to nurse ... Women have not the stamina they once possessed; and I myself know of no greater misery than nursing a child, the physical collapse caused by which is often at the bottom of the drinking habits of which we hear so much.*

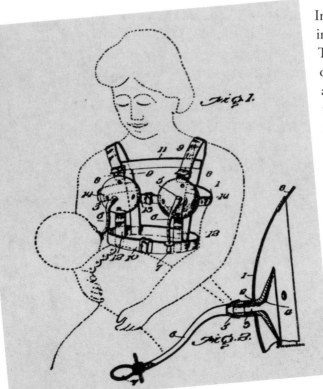

In the early twentieth century, in New Zealand, Sir Frederick Truby King, who also had other rather less helpful ideas about childcare, was a lone voice crying out in the wilderness in support of breastfeeding, and even he went on to invent Karitane, his own 'humanised' milk formula.

A 1910 advertisement shows an 'anti-embarrassment' breastfeeding device for mothers who were still defiantly breastfeeding their children. With a harness that cupped the breasts, and rubber teats attached to the nipples for the baby to suckle on, it was intended to prevent 'exposure of the person' – but must surely have prevented all but the most stubborn mothers breastfeeding. This may seem laughable, but as recently as 2005 a mother was forced out of Hampton Court palace for trying to breastfeed her baby in public. Perhaps she should have been wearing an anti-embarrassment device …

The Cuddle Monsters

Most mothers today feel guilty because they don't spend enough time with their children, but a hundred years ago it was over-affectionate ones who were getting the flak. This quote is from *Psychological Care of Infant and Child* by J.B. Watson, an Edwardian childcare expert:

> *It is a serious question in my mind whether there should be individual homes for children – or even whether children should know their own parents at all. There are undoubtedly much more scientific ways of bringing up children, which will probably mean finer and happier children. I suppose parents want their children to be happy, efficient, and well-adjusted to life.*

Throughout the first half of the twentieth century there was a general trend in science, partly inspired by ideas about hygiene and partly as a reaction to Freud, that encouraged mothers not to cuddle or play with their children too much. Watson was an extreme example of this 'don't touch' school. Truby King, too, didn't believe in spending a lot of time with babies, apart from when they were fed (which was to be done at regular intervals, and never at night).

> *A real Truby King baby … is as full of abounding vitality as the puppy playing in the yard. He sleeps and kicks out of doors as much as the weather allows, and sleeps at night in the airiest bedroom, or on an open*

veranda or porch … After he has gone through his regular morning performance of bathing and being 'held out' [over the potty], and has had breakfast, he sleeps all morning. If he wakes a little before his 2pm meal, all that one knows about it is a suddenly glimpsed chubby little leg or foot waved energetically from his cot for inspection, or a vigorous jerking of his pram.

Truby King babies, of which my mother Jocasta was one (my grandmother, Eileen, was Cambridge-educated and followed fashions in childcare with interest) were meant to spend as much time as possible alone in their cots, playpens and prams, be potty-trained at nine months and never, ever sleep in their mother's bed.

Here is another quote from Watson, in 1928, talking about contact with babies and children:

Nearly all of us have suffered from over-coddling in our infancy. How does it show? It shows in invalidism … coddling is a dangerous experiment … the fact that our children are always crying and always whining shows the unhappy, unwholesome state they are in. There is a sensible way of treating children. Treat them as though they were young adults. Never hug and kiss them, never let them sit on your lap. If you must, kiss them once on the forehead when they say good night. Shake hands with them in the morning … try it out. In a week's time you will be utterly ashamed of the mawkish, sentimental way you have been handling it …

Manuals, Manuals, Manuals

This is Jean Liedloff in her interview with *Touch The Future*, being scathing about the baby-book boom (which didn't stop her writing *The Continuum Concept*).

Here we are, great big grown-up louts in our twenties or thirties reading books about how to take care of babies. I'd be embarrassed to admit to the Indians that our women don't know how to take care of their children until they read instructions written in a book by a man, a man they've never met. The Indians wouldn't have any respect for me. If you were there, you wouldn't either.

When did we become so obsessed with reading manuals? Was it when women lost control of giving birth in the late eighteenth and early nineteenth centuries? They were no longer seen as the 'experts' in mothering and it was time for men to tell them how to do it properly. There is a telling scene in Mary McCarthy's 1953 novel *The Group*, where one of the characters has just had a baby. She doesn't want to breastfeed but her doctor husband insists that she follows his patented breastfeeding routine. He tells her, 'This is no time for personal weakness, you must be an example to modern mothers everywhere.' Presumably he was also thinking about the book deal. Childcare manuals are big business: Dr Spock's *Baby and Child Care* is the best-selling work of non-fiction after the Bible and the collected works of Mao Tse-tung.

But who can blame women for seeking advice from the 'experts' when every day there is a new scare about how they are raising their children? In one week in September I counted twenty-three such stories in the *Daily Mail*. No wonder new mothers want the cool calm voice of authority. In an article in the *Observer* the journalist Miranda Sawyer described how she got into the manual habit after the birth of her son:

Well, many women obsess about getting things right, whether it's this season's layering or a toddler's eating habits. The more checklists or rotas or menus they can stick to, the more ticks they can amass, the more reassured they feel that, yes, it's OK, goals are being achieved, life is under control, everything nasty is at bay because an outfit is planned and bought, an organic meal is prepared and frozen. There are plenty out there willing to exploit that mama-licious anxiety for cold hard cash.

Essential Viewing for New Mums

Thirtysomething: How does Hope look so fabulous seconds after giving birth?

Friends Series Six: In particular, the episode where Rachel's baby won't stop crying.

Shlocky daytime chat shows: However bad you look or feel, the punters on the show will look and feel worse.

Three Men and a Baby: For an effortless feeling of superiority.

Baby Boom: See above.

101 Dalmatians: Even if you are having to sit on a rubber ring at least you haven't given birth to a litter.

And for new dads, *March of the Penguins*: No matter how many times you had to get up in the night, at least you didn't have to stand for nine weeks in Antarctic winds with an egg between your feet.

Such worry fluffing explains the enormous pile of parenting books that most mothers of small children own. In a fit of panic, when my son was 12 days old, I spent a small fortune on seven on Amazon. And every single one gave me different advice ... Even a simple question like where your baby sleeps is fraught with conflict. In your room? Yes, says the World Health Organization. On its own? Yes, says Contented Little Baby *guru-stroke-millionaire Gina Ford ... Should you put your baby in a full-size cot (Gina Ford)? Or a Moses basket (everyone else)? Or with you in your bed (Active-Birth sage Janet Balaskas)? On its back (midwives)? Or its side (other midwives)? Or its front (your mum)?*
(1 OCTOBER 2006)

~
How to Survive the First Six Weeks

What amazed me when I had my first baby was how much emphasis was placed on pregnancy and birth, and how little preparation there was for life after birth. When you're pregnant you can still go to the movies or wash your hair without it being a major logistical exercise. No one tells you that for many new mothers a good day is one where you manage to get dressed before lunchtime.

The first six weeks after you have your baby are known as the 'puerperium' in Latin medical-speak ('around the baby', in case you're wondering), and they have a special name because of the bizarre changes your body will go through during this time. When you lose your placenta you lose a hormone factory that's been a vital part of your life for the last nine months, and the changes can be dramatic and will affect your mood and emotions. It's important to be aware of this or it can come as a bit of a shock.

The Western experience seems to be that after nine months of attention your well-being is of secondary importance; everyone is focused on the baby. It's possible to feel 'What about me?', especially if you had a difficult birth, or are post-operative after a Caesarean section – or if everything went well and people are behaving as if you're 'normal'. This feeling is not new, as was recognised, for example, in Mrs Panton's *The Way They Should Go*, published in 1896:

> *The dreams that a young mother is supposed to dream over the cradle of her newborn baby are about as real as her supposedly passionate desire for children. She dreams principally about herself – she longs to be out of bondage. A little indignant at the manner in which the child engrosses everyone's time and attention, the while she is abjectly terrified of it, and as abjectly afraid that everyone who touches it will do it a mischief … wondering how many more minutes it is going to live. She even wishes she never got married. These thoughts may not be noble, but they are universal, and therefore the girl who finds them agitating her breast need not write herself down a monster – the phase will soon pass.*

Many cultures do recognise that women need a lot of love, attention and rest after giving birth, in order to enjoy the 'babymoon' (a much prettier term than 'puerperium'). Ayurvedic tradition in India encourages a new mother to stay at home and be pampered for the first 22 days post-partum. She is cooked for, visitors are restricted and she is sheltered. In Bali, a woman can't enter her kitchen or wash her hair until the baby's cord stump has fallen off, while the baby is not allowed to touch the ground for the first 105 days of its life, and is carried by members of the family. Most Indonesian women don't leave the family home or resume their regular household duties until the baby is 42 days old.

According to the book of Leviticus, in the Old Testament, a woman was unclean until she had visited the tabernacle, a belief reflected in the custom of 'churching', described in *The Oxford Dictionary of Superstitions*:

The mother never sets about any work until she has been kirked. In the church of Scotland there is no ceremony on the occasion; but the woman, attended by some of her neighbours, goes into church sometimes in service time, but oftener when it is empty, goes out again, surrounds it, refreshes herself at some public house, and then returns home. Before this ceremony she is looked on as unclean, never is permitted to eat with the family; nor will anyone eat of the victuals she has dressed.

Visiting friends and neighbours was also frowned upon until a woman had been churched. Still, at least she had a chance to go to the pub and didn't have to cook …

~ Visitors

In the first place I wish you joy of your Niece, for I was brought to bed of a daughter 5 weeks ago … I don't mention this as one of my diverting adventures, tho I must own that it is not halfe so mortifying here as in England, there being as much difference as there is between a little cold in the head, which sometimes happens here, and the Consumptive Coughs so common in London. No body keeps their house a Month for lying-in, and I am not so fond of any of our Customs to retain them when they are not necessary. I return'd my visits at 3 weeks end, and about 4 days ago cross'd the Sea which divides this place from Constantinople to make a new one, where I had the good fortune to pick up many Curiositys.

This quote is from a letter Lady Mary Wortley Montagu wrote to her sister in the early eighteenth century. The beautiful, aristocratic and witty wife of the ambassador to Turkey – she had eloped with Edward Montagu as a young woman and had nearly been disinherited by her family – was a great mother, and took her children with her on her travels. She was interested in medicine in particular (she mentions cold baths for curing rickets, and inoculated her little boy against smallpox when they were in Turkey). In earlier letters she had described how the Turks allowed women to be visited on 'the day of their Delivery', and how the new mothers returned visits after a fortnight 'set out in their Jewells and new Cloaths', so she obviously felt that the month's lying-in after birth ordained for English women was an imposition.

Here is the Victorian male view of how a new mother should behave after the birth:

> *It is most important, through the whole of the lying-in month, that the body and mind of the patient should be kept perfectly easy. It has been already observed that the lying-in apartment must be kept cool and well ventilated; it must also be kept quiet.*
>
> *In reference to the admission of visitors, in a first confinement, I am always apprehensive of mischief; for it is then that the lying-in room is so attractive. The numerous relatives and friends all eagerly flock to the house, anxious just to see the young mother, and nurse the child. If this anxiety is indulged by the medical man, it never fails to be injurious. It is not uncommon to hear people say, when the mischief is done, 'Oh! We thought her so well that a visit could not possibly be hurtful'. It is always running a most unjustifiable risk; for the very pleasure that the patient experiences in seeing her young friends, under her present circumstances, is alone sufficient so to excite and disturb her system as to be productive of the most unfavourable results. The most perfect quiet and repose, then, are positively necessary to the well-doing of the patient; she must be seen by only one visitor, her medical friend.*

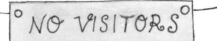

Thus spoke Thomas Bull in his 1877 *Hints to Mothers*. This is a book guaranteed to produce anxiety for women at all stages of their pregnancies, as it routinely threatens dire consequences for anyone who doesn't listen to his advice. As well as starving for the first three days after birth, taking repeated enemas, denying the baby the breast until the milk has come in and remaining in the recumbent position for one month post-delivery (one month!) he suggests total solitary confinement as the best way to deal with post-partum mothers:

> *It is never safe to join the family circle before the expiration of the third week; and the month from delivery having terminated, if all be going on well, the patient may gradually resume her accustomed duties, and go out of doors without risk.*

It worked for me

I had my first baby in a hospital with strict visiting hours. Because it was the first baby in the family for both sets of grandparents everybody wanted to visit all the time. Actually the birth had been quite tricky and I was exhausted, so I was rather relieved when the nurse threw everyone out. I could pretend I didn't want them to go while being secretly delighted that I was going to get some peace and quiet. When you are choosing a hospital, bear this in mind. *Tanya, mother of Jack (4 years) and Rory (2 years)*

It's interesting that what had been a cultural requirement for new mothers in the eighteenth century, for Lady Mary Wortley Montagu and her like, had become a medical necessity for similar ladies by the nineteenth. Even in the twentieth century, there's an expectation that you will slow down to some extent when you've just had your baby. This is Miriam Stoppard's advice:

'*Traditionally, women were not expected to reappear in society until some time after their babies' births. They spent this time regaining their strength. Today we consider it vital to have a period of peace and relaxation in the days immediately following the birth of a baby. It gives both partners a chance to celebrate the birth, welcome and bond with the new baby, and adjust to their new roles as parents … Don't feel you have to entertain. You need to conserve your strength, and being good hosts every afternoon for the first week or so will really wear you out, so don't feel guilty about restricting visiting hours.*'

So that rules out presenting television programmes from your hospital bed like Katie Couric, the celebrated American TV anchor.

Sex Post-baby

Q. I say Doctor, how soon should I start having sex after the birth?
A. A gentleman waits until his wife has left the delivery room.

Sexual emotion of frequent occurrence deteriorates the quality of the milk.

The quotation about sexual emotion comes from *Every Mother's Handbook*, published in the early twentieth century, but the idea that sex is bad for nursing mothers dates back to Galen, a Roman physician who was born in AD 129. This erroneous belief may have led to the eighteenth-century fashion for employing wet nurses for upper-class children.

According to Jewish law a woman who has just given birth should not have sex for 40 days. Many cultures share this traditional ban on sex soon after birth (like the restrictions on household activities, it could be argued that the custom has benefits as well as drawbacks), and until fairly recently sex was prohibited for six weeks after giving birth, for medical reasons. Nowadays, Miriam Stoppard says stopping sex for the first six weeks post-baby is not compulsory, but on the other hand (quite sensibly) you may not want to have sex straight away.

You probably won't be in the mood for making love in the first days, or even weeks, after giving birth, because the sheer physical exhaustion of labor and the drastic changes in your hormone levels after delivery combine to inhibit sexual desire. An initial lack of interest in sex is both natural and desirable ... The arrival of the baby can also have a damp-ening effect on your partner's libido; it is not uncommon for a father to feel a lack of desire.

Cold Feet, the seminal thirty-something 'parents in crisis' drama had a great scene when Pete, the sex-starved new father, finally went to bed with Jenny, who'd had the medical all-clear, and discovered he'd mislaid his libido. It's a good reminder that love, like a baby, doesn't always go by the book …

Naming the Baby

1883 BURNE Shropshire 286–7
The Colliery people … consider it extremely unlucky to mention a child's name before it is christened. The father always 'picks' the name, and often tells it to no one until he whispers it in the godmother's ear on the day of the christening.
THE OXFORD DICTIONARY OF SUPERSTITIONS

In medieval times men waited outside the birth chamber, and when the baby was born they took it to be baptised. First, in a kind of 'express' ceremony at the entrance to the church, the priest threw holy water on the baby and put salt on its mouth, then touched it after spitting on his hands. After this the baby was taken inside the church and baptised by complete submersion in the font (which is why fonts were large in those days). All this was because of the belief that unbaptised babies who died shortly after birth would go to limbo rather than heaven because they had been born with original sin. Baptism cleansed them of this. Babies, said one preacher, 'are symple, withowt gyle, innocent, wythout harme, and all pure wythowt corruption.'

In primitive or traditional cultures naming the baby was often a way of expressing thanks that it had survived its first few weeks, and there is still a celebratory aspect to this. For example, Indonesian mothers enjoy a naming ceremony for the baby and a family feast on the 42nd day of its life – and then return to their household duties. Perhaps celebrities should also wait 42 days before deciding to call their child after a fruit or a borough of New York.

100 MOST POPULAR NAMES FOR GIRLS AND BOYS IN 2006

Girls' names

Olivia	Caitlin	Matilda
Grace	Rebecca	Sienna
Jessica	Georgia	Shannon
Ruby	Lauren	Lilly
Emily	Madison	Madeleine
Sophie	Amber	Zoë
Chloë	Elizabeth	Nicole
Lucy	Eleanor	Eva
Lily	Bethany	Skye
Ellie	Isabel	Amelie
Ella	Paige	Abbie
Charlotte	Scarlett	Harriet
Katie	Alice	Maya
Mia	Imogen	Zara
Hannah	Sophia	Rachel
Amelia	Anna	Francesca
Megan	Lola	Lydia
Amy	Libby	Alicia
Isabella	Maisie	Hollie
Millie	Isobel	Sofia
Evie	Brooke	Alexandra
Abigail	Alisha	Layla
Freya	Tia	Natasha
Molly	Sarah	Mollie
Daisy	Summer	Morgan
Holly	Gracie	Isla
Emma	Faith	Demi
Erin	Courtney	Laura
Isabelle	Niamh	Lara
Poppy	Ava	Tilly
Jasmine	Eve	Martha
Leah	Aimee	Eloise
Keira	Maddison	
Phoebe	Rosie	

Boys' names

Jack	Connor	Mohammad
Thomas	Harrison	Kian
Joshua	Nathan	Bailey
Oliver	Ben	Sam
Harry	Henry	Joel
James	Archie	Leon
William	Edward	John
Samuel	Michael	Robert
Daniel	Aaron	Ellis
Charlie	Muhammed	Joe
Benjamin	Kyle	Luca
Joseph	Noah	Billy
Callum	Oscar	Corey
George	Lucas	Ashton
Jake	Rhys	Evan
Alfie	Bradley	Taylor
Luke	Charles	Christopher
Matthew	Toby	Aidan
Ethan	Louis	Elliot
Lewis	Brandon	Hayden
Jacob	Isaac	Morgan
Mohammed	Reece	Jay
Dylan	Kieran	Dominic
Alexander	Alex	Theo
Ryan	Finlay	Zachary
Adam	Finley	Sean
Tyler	Mason	Sebastian
Harvey	Kai	Reuben
Max	Logan	Andrew
Cameron	Riley	Gabriel
Liam	Freddie	Frederick
Jamie	David	Ewan
Leo	Harley	
Owen	Jayden	

~ Those Baby Blues

Finding yourself in floods of tears after you've had a baby is perfectly normal, but that doesn't make it any easier. I remember I spent more time than my baby crying.

Expert opinion on how to cope with the baby blues is very much 'It's just a phase dear'. This is what Dr Spock had to say about 'The Blue Feeling' in 1957:

The majority of mothers don't get discouraged enough in this period to ever call it depression. You may think it is a mistake to bring up unpleasant things that may never happen. The reason I mention it is that several mothers have told me afterwards, 'I'm sure I wouldn't have been so depressed or discouraged if I had known how common this feeling is. Why, I thought that my whole outlook on life had changed for good and all.' You can face a thing much better if you know that a lot of other people have gone through it, too, and if you know that it's just temporary.

If you begin to feel depressed, try to get some relief from the constant care of the baby in the first month or two, especially if he cries a great deal. Go to a movie, or to the beauty parlor, or to get yourself a new hat or dress. Visit a good friend occasionally. Take the baby along if you can't find anyone to stay with him. Or get your old friends to come and see you. All of these are tonics … If the depression does not lift in a few days or it is becoming worse, you should promptly get in touch with a psychiatrist, through your regular doctor.

Interestingly, advice for mild post-baby depression has not changed much. The following advice from Miriam Stoppard suggests a regimen not very different from Dr Spock's, although she does skip the bit about a new hat. However, the emphasis on fresh air is almost Edwardian, and I like the advice telling you on the one hand to avoid snacking on chocolate while on the other to avoid dieting. The maternity nurse I had with my eldest practically force-fed me chocolate biscuits saying the baby would get better-quality milk – so there you are.

> ***Rest as much as possible.*** *Being tired definitely makes depression worse and harder to cope with. Catnap during the day, and if possible, get someone to help with night feedings.*

> ***Maintain a proper diet.*** *Eat plenty of fruit or raw vegetables, don't snack or binge on chocolate, candy or cookies. Eat little and often. Do not go on a strict diet.*

> ***Get gentle exercise.*** *Give yourself a rest from being indoors or taking care of the baby. A brisk walk in the fresh air can work wonders.*

> ***Avoid major upheavals.*** *Don't start a new job, move to a new home, or redecorate.*

> ***Try not to worry unduly.*** *Aches and pains are common after childbirth, and more so if you are depressed. Try to take them in your stride; they will almost certainly fade away as soon as you can relax.*

> ***Be kind to yourself.*** *Don't worry about not keeping the house spotless or letting household tasks lapse …*

> ***Talk about your feelings.*** *Don't bottle up your concerns; this can make matters worse. Talk to others, particularly your partner.*

There isn't much the experts can say on the subject that is new, except that nowadays it is taken more seriously.

~ Postnatal Depression

The author William Makepeace Thackeray was married to Isabella (I have a special interest in her, as our families are connected through the Traill family). In August 1840 she wrote this letter to her mother-in-law:

> *I feel myself excited, my strength is not great and my head flies away with me as if it were a balloon. This is mere weakness and a walk will set me right but in case there should be incoherence in my letter you will know what to attribute it to … I think my fears imaginary and exaggerated and that I am a coward by nature.*

This was the only time she was able to describe her illness. Thackeray described it later:

> *At first she was violent, then she was indifferent, now she is melancholy and silent and we are glad of it … She knows everybody and recollects things but in a stunned confused sort of way. She kissed me at first very warmly and with tears in her eyes, then she went away from me, as if she felt she was unworthy of having such a God of a husband.*

It's interesting that Thackeray interprets Isabella's actions as feeling she was unworthy to have 'such a God of a husband'. Apparently many women felt worse when they saw their husbands because they associated them with the pregnancy and childbirth that had caused them so much suffering. Sadly, Isabella never recovered and had to be cared for by a nurse, although unlike many Victorian women she was not sent to an asylum. Nor was she locked away in the nursery with wall coverings that had a mind of their own, as happened to the heroine of Charlotte Perkins Gilman's psychological horror story *The Yellow Wallpaper*.

Of course it is only nervousness. It does weigh on me so not to do my duty in any way!

I meant to be such a help to John, such a real rest and comfort, and here I am a comparative burden already!

Nobody would believe what an effort it is to do what little I am able, – to dress and entertain, and other things.

It is fortunate Mary is so good with the baby. Such a dear baby!

And yet I CANNOT be with him, it makes me so nervous.

I suppose John never was nervous in his life. He laughs at me so about this wall-paper!

Charlotte Perkins Gilman eventually divorced her husband and went on to earn a living for herself and her daughter. Her explanation as to why she wrote *The Yellow Wallpaper* shows how unhelpful current medical advice was for her after her breakdown (which coincided with the birth of her daughter in 1885):

For many years I suffered from a severe and continuous nervous breakdown tending to melancholia – and beyond. During about the third year of this trouble I went, in devout faith and some faint stir of hope, to a noted specialist in nervous diseases, the best known in the country. This wise man put me to bed and applied the rest cure, to which a still-good physique responded so promptly that he concluded there was nothing much the matter with me, and sent me home with solemn advice to 'live as domestic a life as far as possible,' to 'have but two hours' intellectual life a day,' and 'never to touch pen, brush, or pencil again' as long as I lived. This was in 1887.

I went home and obeyed those directions for some three months, and came so near the borderline of utter mental ruin that I could see over.

Then, using the remnants of intelligence that remained, and helped by a wise friend, I cast the noted specialist's advice to the winds and went to work again ... ultimately recovering some measure of power.

Being naturally moved to rejoicing by this narrow escape, I wrote The Yellow Wallpaper, *with its embellishments and additions, to carry out the ideal (I never had hallucinations or objections to my mural decorations) and sent a copy to the physician who so nearly drove me mad. He never acknowledged it.*

In 1831, in *A Practical Compendium of Midwifery*, the London obstetrician Robert Gooch gave an account of post-natal depression or 'puerperal insanity':

Nervous irritation is very common after delivery, more especially among fashionable ladies, and this may exist in any degree between mere peevishness and downright madness. Some women, though naturally amiable and good tempered, are so irritable after delivery that their husbands cannot enter their bed-rooms without getting a certain lecture; others are thoroughly mad.

With his comment about 'fashionable' ladies, Gooch resurrects an idea current even in the nineteenth century, that middle- and upper-class women

---

It worked for me

Adelaide first suffered from postnatal depression when she returned to work five-and-a-half months after having Millie. She took time off and eventually worked part-time four days a week, and has since recovered from her depression.

'It's the difference between the concept of having a baby and the reality.' She recommends 'getting out of the house and doing something normal. Take the pressure off yourself. You're dictated to by so many people about what is right for the baby. You're scared witless with a new baby, but trust your instincts and don't listen to everybody. Four women out of five from my antenatal class couldn't breastfeed, so don't feel bad if you can't. Don't expect to look a million dollars after you've had your baby, forget about housework and let yourself recover from the sleep deprivation.' ***Adelaide, mother of Millie (10 months)*** were somehow more vulnerable, or prone to making a fuss, than their sturdier working-class counterparts. They were criticised for taking to the sofa during pregnancy and for being irritable after birth – surely every woman's privilege, even today!

The New Father

Now that fathers are expected to take an equal share in parenting (that's the idea, anyway) the experts have found a whole new audience. Although the *Yummy Daddy Handbook* does not exist at the time of writing, it can only be a matter of time. But some new fathers may hanker after the days when, according to the *1909 Book of the Home*: 'A father's main duties following the birth are to register the child's birth and to make sure it is inoculated against disease.'

Only a generation ago, fathers were being cajoled rather than ordered into the nursery. Here is Dr Spock on the role of new dads:

> *Some fathers have been brought up to think that the care of babies and children is the mother's job entirely. But a man can be a warm father and a real man at the same time ... Of course, I don't mean that the father has to give just as many bottles or change just as many diapers as the mother. But it's fine for him to do these things occasionally. He might make the formula on Sunday. If the baby is on a 2 a.m. bottle in the early weeks, when the mother is still pretty tired, this is a good feeding for the father to take over. It's nice for him, if he can, to go along to the doctor's office for the baby's regular visits ... Of course, there are some fathers who get goose flesh at the very idea of helping to take care of a baby, and there's no good to be gained by trying to force them.*

In nearly three hundred pages of advice, Thomas Bull's nineteenth-century

Hints to Mothers makes no mention of fathers, and nor do they figure in the index. Back in those days, the father featured mainly offstage, the feared patriarch of the household rather than the 'hands-on dad' we expect today. In the eighteenth century Jean Jacques Rousseau, who introduced the idea that a child was an innocent being who needed to grow up among the wilds of nature, actually gave all his children away to an orphanage rather than allow them to cramp his style.

In 1957, as the above quote makes clear, men were still expected to do very little in comparison to their wives. 'It's nice for him, if he can … it's fine for him to do these things occasionally … ' You can see that Spock expects the little woman to do the heavy lifting of childcare, and that dad's involvement is more along the lines of a hobby. In 2006, with 180,000 or more fathers looking after their children full-time, and an increasing number doing so part-time, things look quite different. An Equal Opportunities Commission survey of new fathers found:

'Almost eight out of ten working fathers revealed that they would be happy to stay at home and look after their baby, while almost nine out of ten men felt as confident as their partner when caring for their child. In general, seven out of ten dads wanted to be more involved with caring for their child.'

So there you have it. Just as women are starting to crumble under the pressures of 'having it all', men are willing and ready to step in.

It worked for me

I hadn't realised how much I would change after the birth of my son. I had my two-week paternity leave and I loved every moment of it. I felt increasingly sad about being at work full-time. So my wife and I decided to make some changes. We now both work four days a week and spend the other day with the baby. It caused a bit of fuss at work but it was the best decision I ever made. *Dan, father of Alex (8 months)*

And finally, here is a poem by Gabriela Mistral that all new parents will appreciate:

If You'll Just
Go To Sleep

The blood red rose
I gathered yesterday
And the fire and cinnamon
Of the carnation,

Bread baked with
Anise seed and honey,
And a fish in a bowl
That makes a glow:

All this is yours
Baby born of woman
If you'll just
Go to sleep.

A rose I say!
I say a carnation!
Fruit, I say!
And I say honey!

A fish that glitters!
And more, I say –
If you will only
Sleep till day.

GABRIELA MISTRAL

sleep!

milk

-3-

Food For Thought

*Anyone who has had a baby knows
that the reality of trying to breastfeed is
totally different from the concept.*

A little child born yesterday
A thing on mother's milk and kisses fed
HOMER, 'HYMN TO HERMES'

Trying to manoeuvre a tiny, wriggling, sometimes very reluctant human being into the right position, while anxiously scrutinising its little face to see if it is correctly 'latching on', is very different from the cheery practice sessions with dolls you might have been introduced to in breastfeeding classes. Not to mention the undignified breastfeeding paraphernalia you are lumbered with: breast pads, breast pumps and ridiculous 'nursing' tops. As the heroine of *The Rise and Fall of a Yummy Mummy* discovers at a nightclub, breastfeeding, at least in the early days, is hard to reconcile with feeling sexy:

'*The man is drooling, hopping closer, his eyes focused on my swollen cleavage. I feel myself ripen with the attention. Getting bumped by bottoms in low-rise jeans, he bends down and picks something up off the floor, a white disc. Not looking at it, he passes it to me smiling. "You've dropped something … " Oh my God! Squatting in his hand, domed, sodden, is my breast pad.*'

Still, breastfeeding is the orthodoxy (in theory, if not in practice) nowadays and many women persevere, and even start to feel close to those beatific mothers in the manuals. Perhaps not quite as ecstatic as one eighteenth-century commentator, William Buchan, would have it in *Domestic Medicine*:

> ... *the thrilling sensations that accompany the act of giving suck can be conceived only by those who have felt them, while the mental rapture of a fond mother at such moments are far beyond the powers of description or fancy.*

However, breastfeeding has not always been popular and has gone in and out of fashion just like anything else in childcare. I've already talked about Queen Victoria and her dislike of nursing, and the Edwardian lady who compared breastfeeding women to cows, but there have always been different schools of thought in this area and (of course) very different advice for parents – for example, this from the eighteenth century, in Hugh Smith's *Letters to Married Women*:

> *Believe it not when it is insinuated that your bosoms are less charming for having a dear little cherub at your breast.*

During the eighteenth century, it was common for working- and middle-class mothers to breastfeed, while aristocrats and wealthier women sent their children to a wet nurse. These were seen as the two most desirable options, while 'hand feeding' or artificial feeding was a dangerous business because of difficulties with hygiene and having access to fresh milk (it was only the French who solved this problem by getting animals to suckle foundling babies). It was probably tradition, and perhaps the worry that their husbands wouldn't find them attractive, that made upper-class women choose not to breastfeed. This had a bad effect on the health of their children, who were recognised as not always being robust.

However, the influence of thinkers like Jean Jacques Rousseau, the author of *Emile* (which encouraged breastfeeding and education through 'nature') and purported father of the French Revolution (which attacked wet-nursing along with other aristocratic practices), meant forward-thinking women such as Mary Wollstonecraft began to rebel against the custom, and it became positively fashionable to breastfeed. Rather as in the case of 'eco' mums and dads today, there was a cultural change at work, reflected in Wollstonecraft's *Vindication of the Rights of Women*:

> *There are many husbands so devoid of sense and parental affection that, during the first effervescence of voluptuous fondness, they refuse to let their wives suckle their children …*
> *Nature has so wisely ordered things that did women suckle their children, they would preserve their own health, and there would be such an interval between the birth of each child, that we should seldom see a houseful of babies.*

However, this Romantic approach to breastfeeding was wavering by the mid-nineteenth century, and the pendulum was soon swinging in the other direction as the Victorian mother replaced her eighteenth-century predecessor. After months of 'confinement', a woman could hardly have welcomed the breastfeeding regime which, it was widely agreed, meant a bland, starchy diet, moderate exercise, a limited social life and no stimulants such as alcohol. Even strong emotions were to be avoided, as Lydia Child advises in *The Mother's Book*:

> *Avoid all over-heating from running, dancing, excessive fatigue &c; likewise the indulgence of violent passions and emotions.*

She warns that children can have convulsions if they are breastfed in these conditions – enough to put anybody off!

Mrs Beeton was also biased against breastfeeding; in her *Book of Household Management* she says that an artificial diet is often superior and makes it clear that by comparison the period when a woman breastfeeds is one of 'privation and penance':

The nine or twelve months a woman usually suckles must be, to some extent, to most mothers, a period of privation and penance, and unless she is deaf to the cries of her baby, and insensible to its kicks and plunges, and will not see in such muscular evidences the griping pains that rack her child, she will avoid every article that can remotely affect the little being who draws its sustenance from her. She will see that the babe is acutely affected by all that in any way influences her, and willingly curtail her own enjoyments, rather than see her infant rendered feverish, irritable, and uncomfortable.

As the best tonic, then, and the most efficacious indirect stimulant that a mother can take at such times, there is no potation equal to porter and stout, or, what is better still, an equal part of porter and stout.

It worked for me

At the hospital, I was having problems with my milk supply and they put me on a pump and all the milk started coming out – that really helped. After that, I found breastfeeding easy and didn't bother using the pump except on a few occasions when I wanted to go out. Looking back, I think it helps to get babies into a routine – I kept thinking Max was hungry when he wasn't. If you feed them constantly, they're never properly hungry. We used to wake Max at 11 p.m. for his feed and then he'd sleep through till 6 a.m. When he was six months old, we knocked out that 11 o'clock feed and now he sleeps right through. Other tips: don't go away from your baby for so long that your breasts explode! Make sure you drink a lot of water if you are worried about your milk supply. And make sure you've got a comfortable chair. I found a breastfeeding pillow very helpful as it stopped me getting backache. *Chloe, mother of Max (1 year)*

By the early twentieth century the breastfeeding heroine of Mary Wollstone-craft's day had become the 'common or ordinary "cow"' of Mrs Panton's *The Way They Should Go*. Bottled milk was seen as more hygienic, and much more modern. This emphasis on 'healthiness' of mind and body might have been a reaction against Freud's insights into the physicality of breastfeeding:

> *No one who has seen a baby sinking back satiated from the breast and falling asleep with flushed cheeks and a blissful smile can escape the reflection that this picture persists as a prototype of the expression of sexual satisfaction in later life.*

Heaven knows what early childcare theorists would have made of the 'orgasmic breastfeeding' school!

As I mentioned earlier, it was Sir Frederick Truby King, and his band of acolytes, who led the pro-breastfeeding crusade in the early twentieth century, in New Zealand and later in Britain. A 'typical admission' at his Mothercraft Training Society in London in 1918 included 'Baby Harbor'. As a result of attending the society's classes, Baby Harbor's mother, aged 40, was able to breastfeed her although she had not been able to do so with her previous seven children. Her husband, a carter in Vauxhall, apparently responded by saying, 'My word, mother, you're a real mother this time and no mistake!' However, by sticking to the four-hourly feeds that were prescribed at the time, rather than the three-hourly ones that Chavasse, for example, had proposed in his *Advice to Mothers* in the late nineteenth century, Truby King made life difficult for quite a few mothers and babies, as it was difficult to stimulate enough milk at four-hourly intervals, and mothers were driven to supplement theirs with formulae and eventually give up breastfeeding.

It's interesting that someone as obsessed as Truby King was with regular feeding for babies was famously irregular when it came to his own meals. He ate at unconventional times, even when dining out. He also dressed oddly and could be absent-minded (he once went to a party at Buckingham Palace wearing woollen gloves with a silk top hat).

It worked for me

My baby was very small when she was born because of my pre-eclampsia. She was term and did not need any special care but she was tiny, so she could not really manage without a lot of fairly frequent feeding. This formed most of our initial habits.

I became used to lots of night feeds, lots of day feeds, lots of feeds – and then bad sleep, sleeping together, eventually in my bed – all the things that I knew were not altogether in our mutual interests.

We were champion breastfeeders as a pair (me doing the breasts – she doing the feeding), but in a way that's probably not easy for some mums to emulate. I would certainly have struggled if she was a second child, as another small person to attend to would have made our sort of feeding difficult to sustain.

I also believe that in the end our chaotic initial habits formed the basis of all the difficulties we had with weaning. It was so awful and only happened just before her second birthday.

With every child there are pros and cons to every way of doing just about everything. I am very grateful that we did manage to breastfeed as well as we did – I think it helped to keep minor illnesses to a minimum initially – but it did not stop her getting pneumococcal meningitis at 11 months (she became ill before the vaccination programme started). Perhaps she recovered as well as she did in part because she was breastfed throughout all her hospitalisation and treatment. Most likely we were just very lucky and exceptionally well cared for by the unit that looked after us.

In the end I think it will define our relationship in some subtle way for ever, a bond of necessity and comfort and connection that is both work-a-day and red carpet. *Mary-Anne, mother of Lisa (2 ¾ years)*

The emphasis on regular feeding changed as time went on and 'demand feeding' became more popular, so in the 1950s some women were having trouble with exhaustion caused by not sticking to a routine, as a study by Linda Bryder shows:

> *In Britain the Mothercraft Training Society reported a recent admission to its hospital section, 'Elizabeth House': 'This mother had practised "demand feeding" and had given twelve feeds in 24 hours to the utter exhaustion of herself and the baby, which has one thinking there is something to be said for regular feeding after all!' One mother explained, 'We used to tide our babies over till the feed was due by drinks of water and a cuddle; they very soon were gently trained to wake at the arranged times. Therefore we and our babies were happy in a secure routine; we both knew where we were, and liked it.'*

However, the norm in the 1950s and 1960s, in the United Kingdom as well as the United States, was bottle feeding. In *Feeding in Infancy and Early Childhood*, published in the 1950s, Ursula James (a paediatrician and physician as well as a medical director for the Violet Melchett Mothercraft Centre) laments:

> *Breast milk is the ideal food for the baby in the first few months, and breast feeding should be easy and pleasurable both to the mother and the child. It is sad, therefore, that the incidence of breast feeding is so low, and that so many mothers, for a variety of reasons, do not want to feed their babies. Some mothers are determined never to breast feed, but the majority give it up on account of delay in lactation, pain during feeding, or difficulty in getting the baby to take the breast.*

It took quite a lot of consciousness-raising among the hippy and intellectual types in the 1970s to swing the pendulum back once more. In *The Children of the Dream* Bruno Bettelheim, a contemporary commentator, blames bottle feeding for alcoholism and drug abuse in later life:

> *It (bottle feeding) also made a fetish out of cleanliness, and maybe all the washing and scrubbing has further reduced the pleasure we take in our body and in life.*
>   *Certainly, before bottle feeding, mothers had no choice but to let the*

*infant suck pleasurably from her body, and in the absence of 'baby foods',
this tended to go on for a considerable time ... A great deal of modern
drug and sex behaviour has its roots in the desperate effort to set things
aright – to give the pleasure principle a belated chance to assert itself,
after denying it too early.*

Nowadays, there are some, like Julie Burchill in the *Mail on Sunday*, who
think the swing to breastfeeding has gone too far:

*The New Age recipe for bringing up baby – carry it about with you
constantly and breastfeed it till it can open beercans with its teeth and
have it sleep between you and hubby till it reaches voting age – seems to
me disastrous for a romantic and happy marriage.*

*The Born Again Cows who advise such a regime may well be
responsible for a generation of split families ten years from now. For
nothing turns a man off faster than making him feel he is married to
a womb rather than a woman.*

(26 AUGUST 1990)

~
The Departure of the Wet Nurse

Thus in the anxious time, which Pierre would never forget, after the birth of their first child, when they tried three different wetnurses for the delicate baby and Natasha fell ill with worry, Pierre one day told her of Rousseau's views (with which he was in complete agreement) of how unnatural and deleterious it was to have wetnurses at all. When the next baby was born, in spite of vigorous opposition from her mother, the doctors and even from her husband himself – who were all against her nursing the baby, which to them was something unheard of and pernicious – she insisted on having her own way, and after that nursed all her children herself.

LEO TOLSTOY, *WAR AND PEACE*

Chuse one of middle age, not old nor young,
Nor plump, nor slim her make, but firm and strong:
Upon her cheek, let health refulgent glow
In vivid colours, that good-humour shew:
Long be her arms, and broad her ample chest;
Her neck be finely turn'd, and full her breast:
Let the twin hills be white as mountain snow,
Their swelling veins with circling juices flow;
Each in a well projecting nipple end,
And milk in copious streams, from these descend:
Remember too, the whitest milk you meet,
Of grateful flavour, pleasing taste, and sweet,
Is always best; and if it strongly scent
The air, some latent ill the vessels vent.

Judging by these sixteenth-century instructions in *St Marthe's Poedotrophia,* selecting a wet nurse must have been one of the oddest kinds of job interview imaginable. But employers had to be careful, as John Roberton makes clear in *On the Duties and Qualifications of a Wet-Nurse*, in the early nineteenth century, with his warnings of immoral, mercenary and even syphilitic wet nurses:

> *Connected with the choosing of a nurse are both difficulties and dangers. In this country, the class of persons from which she is commonly selected, contains many, particularly the unmarried part, whose moral character is doubtful; and even the married are mostly mercenary, or extremely poor; circumstances, either of which detracts from the best qualities of a nurse.*
>
> *In the choice of a nurse, as in that of other servants, caution and strict scrutiny are necessary, with this difference, that a correct knowledge of the state of her health is indispensable. Upon this point no evidence should satisfy, except a professional opinion; for it is certain that infants have been destroyed by disease taken from a syphilitic wet-nurse; and the bare possibility of such a calamity should excite parents to the utmost vigilance. It lately fell to the lot of the writer to be consulted in a case of this kind. The nurse, a married woman, became infected, as was said, by her husband. However that might be, the infant in her charge, a fine girl of six months old, perished from the complaint after severe and protracted sufferings.*

Roberton also supplies what sounds like a disgusting recipe for a wet nurse who is having trouble with her milk supply. Ale, as usual, figures prominently:

> *Dr. Struve's ale posset is said to answer excellently. 'Two parts of rich cow's milk are placed over a slow fire; when it begins to boil, one part of well fermented mild ale is added, and the whole gently boiled for another minute. This mixture should be drunk cold.'*

Despite wet nurses' lack of moral fibre, children often became very attached to theirs, perhaps because they sometimes lived with them for several years, and reunion with their mothers became difficult.

Wet nurses were still around in the nineteenth century – Mrs Beeton has instructions as to how to accommodate and look after one, and warns mothers that the nurses may give the children opiates in order to get a good night's sleep. However, this ancient role for women was on its way out, and the wet nurse survived in the twentieth century only in the depersonalised form of the 'breast milk bank'.

'Bringing up Baby by Hand': Artificial Milk

Food for a Young Infant. – Take of fresh cow's milk 1 tablespoonful, and mix with 2 tablespoonsful of hot water; sweeten with loaf-sugar as much as may be agreeable. This quantity is sufficient for once feeding a new-born infant; and the same quantity may be given every 2 or 3 hours – not oftener – till the mother's breast afford the natural nourishment.

With the growing ambivalence about breastfeeding during the nineteenth century, substitutes became more popular. One alternative, like the one above from *The Ladies' New Book of Cookery*, was animal milk that had been adapted through various treatments, although in the eighteenth century French children drank straight from the goat (or sheep), as John Roberton later recorded in *Observations on the Mortality and Physical Management of Children* (see opposite).

In 1878, in *Advice to a Mother*, Chavasse gives a recipe for cows' milk adapted for babies. It sounds relatively harmless apart from the undesirable salt:

'An instance is mentioned, in an early volume of the Annual Register, of an infant that lost its mother on ship-board and was suckled by a goat. By some French writers the sheep is particularly recommended for this purpose. "The great advantage of this method of nursing infants having determined the Governors of the Hospital at Aix to adopt it, one might see each sheep, at the hour of suckling, recognize the nursling confided to her, shew it signs of great attachment, and put herself in the most favourable position for yielding her suck."'

JOHN ROBERTON

New milk, the produce of ONE healthy cow; Warm water, of each, equal parts; Table salt, a few grains – a small pinch; Lump sugar, a sufficient quantity, to slightly sweeten it.

Sugar was often added to a baby's food or drink:

A small quantity of sugar in an infant's food is requisite, sugar being nourishing and fattening, and making cow's milk to resemble somewhat in its properties human milk; but, bear in mind, it must be used sparingly. Much sugar cloys the stomach, weakens the digestion, produces acidity, sour belchings, and wind. Shakespeare: 'Things sweet to taste, prove in digestion sour.'

Other drinks offered to children varied wildly over the years but the following, from Roberton's advice on wet nurses, gives an idea of what they were like:

The kinds of beverage suitable for children may be enumerated in three words, – water, milk, whey. Wine, in some instances, is necessary as a tonic. Spirits, in every form, are to be utterly prohibited; as also, in general, are fermented liquors.

With respect to the infusions of tea and coffee, they would be highly improper, if given alone; but when largely diluted with milk, they are perfectly harmless. In general, tea is much relished by children; perhaps not the less, from its furnishing the usual apology for those noisy migrations, which so frequently take place, from the nursery to the family table.

Recipes for babies' milk became more and more complicated, and by the late nineteenth century manufacturers had spotted the gap in the market for ready-made children's food and drink. As the www.babybottle-museum.co.uk website describes, one enterprising inventor, Justus von Liebig, marketed his 'perfect' infant food in 1867. It was soon followed by a host of imitators.

His 'formula' was a mixture of wheat flour, cow's milk and malt flour cooked with bicarbonate of potash to reduce the flour's acidity. It was first sold as a liquid but later marketed as an entirely farinaceous powder. 'Patent' or 'instant' baby foods manufactured by Nestlé, and Horlicks contained dried cow's milk with starch or malt and Mellin's Food was made with desiccated malt extract. A final group of foods of pure cereal origin was represented by brands such as Imperial Grain, Eskay's Food, and Robinson's Patent Barley.

Nestlé, Robinson and Horlicks are still around today (like Karitane, Truby King's 'humanised milk') – a testament to the enduring nature of childhood brands, or to the marketing muscle of these corporations. The baby-food and drink giants soon began advertising, for example by giving away free

It worked for me

Babies are always rougher to manage between 4 p.m. and midnight. I found on the worst days Lisa was calm until about 3.45 p.m. at the earliest, and she would always be calmer after midnight. For this reason, lots of breastfeeding mums use a bottle of formula some time in the evening. This fills their little babies up and takes about four hours of fussing out of their days. The only downside is that if you have gone to the trouble of breastfeeding in the first place, you are running the risk of your baby developing a cows' milk allergy.

A few mums I know have toddlers who have developed cows' milk allergies (which they mostly get over) from too early an exposure to formula. The whole point of breastfeeding with respect to allergies is that if you are going to get any protection against them, you need to avoid interrupting breastfeeding regularly with formula.

Of course, lots of children get allergies irrespective of breastfeeding and lots of them do not get allergies from one or two bottles of formula a day – but the motivation to avoid allergies through breastfeeding requires an understanding that you have to get used to those fussy evenings. *Mary-Anne, mother of Lisa (2 ¾ years)*

samples, just as they have been accused of doing in developing countries today, but for most of the time they were careful to promote their products as 'equal to' breast milk rather than better.

By the early twentieth century, there were developments that made it a lot easier for mothers who chose to bottle feed. They could, for example, get milk from 'milk depots' that guaranteed clean milk for babies, although the doctors who ran them did not advise everyone to switch to formula. Dr George McCleary's depot, set up in Battersea, London, in 1903, dispensed clean and cheap milk to mothers (but only if they were able to give a good reason for abandoning breastfeeding).

As a result of the invention of vulcanised rubber in the 1840s, teats eventually became more hygienic and comfortable. Mass production of the bottles also began in the mid-nineteenth century. They were usually based on a 'torpedo' or banjo shape. A glass internal tube was attached to a black rubber tube and ended in a bone mouth-shield and rubber teat. Even at the time they were condemned as unhygienic and were given the catchy nickname 'murder baby bottles', but they were used until the 1920s. One reason for their popularity was that babies could be left to feed by themselves – great if you were of the 'don't touch' school of baby nursing.

The double-ended baby feeder was invented by Allen and Hanbury in 1894. It had a teat at one end and a valve at the other, enabling the flow of milk to be controlled and disposing of the dangerous long feeding tube, and was much easier to clean than the older bottles. The improved 1900 model of the 'Allenbury' sold well into the 1950s, although it was during this decade that the narrow-necked heat-resistant upright Pyrex models became popular. Finally, in the 1960s, these were replaced by wide-necked bottles, following the lead of the United States (where bottle feeding and formula were far more popular than breastfeeding throughout the whole of the twentieth century). Wide-necked bottles now come in a multitude of colours, sizes and models, with plastic replacing the glass.

~
Pap and Pap Boats

In the Middle Ages babies were often fed with a cow's horn that had a scrap of soft leather tied to it, while in the seventeenth century leather or wood feeding bottles were used. These were later made in pewter and many examples can still be seen today. They were usually flask-shaped with a screw on top. They were unhygienic and impossible to clean properly, and this, combined with the low nutritional value of the artificial food that was given to babies, must have had a lot to do with the high mortality rates in under-twos.

In *Letters to Married Women*, Hugh Smith related the annual number of births registered in the City of London for each of the ten years from 1762 to 1771 to the annual number of burials of children. He discovered that almost half the children were dead within two years and blamed this on feeding techniques:

> *It is well known that the thrush and watery gripes generally terminate their existence in the early months … The thrush and watery gripes are, in the author's opinion, artificial diseases, and both of them totally occasioned by improper food, such as all kinds of pap, whether made from flour, bread, or biscuit; they all cause too much fermentation in an infant's stomach, and irritate their tender bowels beyond what Nature can support … Let me then intreat those who are desirous of rearing their children, not to rob them of their natural breast. Would they wish them to be healthy and beautiful, let such mothers give suck: for even wet-nurses, we shall find, are very little to be depended upon.*

Thomas Bull, in the nineteenth century, is similarly unenthusiastic about hand feeding, and recommends asses' milk as the best substitute:

> *Extreme delicacy of constitution, diseased condition of the frame, defective*

secretion of milk, and other causes, may forbid the mother suckling her child; and unless she can perform this office with safety to herself and benefit to her infant, she ought not to attempt it. In this case a young and healthy wet-nurse is the best substitute; but even this resource is not always attainable. Under these circumstances the child may be brought up on an artificial diet – 'by hand', as it is popularly called. To accomplish this, however, with success, requires the most careful attention on the part of the parent. It is at all times attended with risk; particularly in large cities … In some respects, however, the milk of the woman is most similar to the milk of the ass, and in the early months, accordingly, we find it the most suitable artificial food that can be chosen.

Chavasse explained why gruels are a bad idea for newborns:

An infant, who, for two or three days, is kept from the breast, and who is fed upon gruel, generally becomes feeble, and frequently, at the end of that time, will not take the nipple at all. Besides, there is a thick cream (similar to the bestings of a cow), which, if not drawn out by the child, may cause inflammation and gathering of the bosom, and, consequently, great suffering to the mother. Moreover, placing him early to the breast, moderates the severity of the mother's after pains, and lessens the risk of her flooding. A new-born babe must not have gruel given to him, as it disorders the bowels, causes a disinclination to suck, and thus makes him feeble.

Pap boats or cups were also used in the eighteenth and nineteenth centuries. They were easier to clean than bottles, so probably less dangerous, and could be made in silver (usually as christening gifts), Staffordshire ceramic or even Wedgwood china. Suckling bottles were originally made of ceramic, and eventually of glass. The teat was often a piece of leather or cloth, or even a preserved cow's teat.

According to the baby bottle museum website:

The term 'pap', allegedly derived from the Scandinavian for the sound made when a baby opens his mouth for nourishment, was probably introduced before its first recordings in literature in the mid 18th century. Recipes for pap usually called for bread, flour and water. A more nourishing mixture, 'panada,' was a pap base with added butter and milk, or cooked in broth as a milk substitute. Variations on the ingredients included Lisbon sugar, beer, wine, raw meat juices and Castile soap. Drugs were sometimes added to 'soothe the baby'.

I don't much like the sound of the Castile soap, not to mention the drugs! Slowly, the use of pap boats declined and bottles began to take over as artificial milk and bottle feeding became more popular.

Feeding by the Clock: the Schedule

There is a great deal of angst over vaccinations, sleeping patterns and nutrition nowadays, but for many years another concern has been how often to feed babies. This wasn't really perceived as a problem while women were mainly breastfeeding: they probably fed their children on demand, or slotted them into the household routine, without being too stressed about it. But when foundling hospitals were established in Britain in the eighteenth century, doctors tried to work out how infants should be fed and the idea of a regular pattern of feeding began to emerge. Whenever babies were given over to the care of people not in the family, whether the carers were eighteenth-century foundling hospitals, nineteenth-century nannies or twentieth-century maternity wards, theories of how – and when – to feed them began to develop.

Truby King rescued babies who were not thriving at home and took them into the hospitals he founded to recover on his regimen of feeding and sleeping

'Fond and foolish over-indulgence,
mismanagement, and "spoiling" may be as
harmful to an infant as callous neglect or
intentional cruelty. The "can't-be-so-cruel"
mother or nurse, who won't bring herself to
wake the baby a few times, if needed, in
order to establish regular feeding habits;
or who weakly gratifies every whim of herself
and the child, rather than allow either
to suffer temporary discomfort for the
sake of permanent health and happiness –
such a woman is really cruel, not kind.
To save a lusty, honest cry she will pacify an
infant with a "comforter", or with food given
at wrong times, and may thus ruin the
child in the first month of life, making him
a delicate, fretful, irritable, nervous,
dyspeptic little tyrant who will yell and
scream, day or night, if not soothed and
cuddled without delay.'

TRUBY KING

'by the book'. His insistence on a four-hourly feeding schedule was based on observing cows and calves. Undoubtedly, he saved many lives, as the children he helped were often being fed nutritionally unhelpful food (such as crushed 'wine biscuits'). Also, the Plunket nurses who helped to spread his methods in New Zealand did a lot to help mothers, as did the Mothercraft Training Societies he founded in Britain. Truby King's methods were slow to catch on in the United Kingdom, but my grandmother, Eileen, was a keen acolyte by the 1940s and brought up my mother, and her sisters and brother, on his system. His theories were based on discoveries about hygiene, and a desire for children to be sturdy and self-reliant, able to spend time on their own while their mothers got on with household tasks (see previous page).

What would Truby King have made of modern manuals, which confidently state that a newborn baby cannot be 'spoilt'? It's lucky we've also disposed of a few of his other ideas, such as the proposition in *The Evils of Cram* that studying impairs the fertility of teenage girls …

Overfeeding, as well as underfeeding, was something he was very concerned to avoid by timing feeds correctly:

> *Maternal instinct does not tell the human mother how long or how often she should suckle her baby. Yet prevention of overfeeding on the one hand and underfeeding on the other, is supremely important. Overfeeding in a breast-fed baby may be recognised by excessive gain in weight, 'putting up' of feed, frequent relaxed motions, restlessness and colic.*

It worked for me

Kerry kept Henry and Penny in bed with her during their first years, after reading *Three in a Bed* by Deborah Jackson, and says it was much easier. 'I was able to feed them lying down instead of having to get up in the night, which is so much harder. It all felt much more natural and I felt easier having the children near me.' *Kerry, mother of Henry (5 years) and Penny (3 years)*

Today the battle over the timing of feeds still rages. Demand feed your baby, or try to get him into a routine? For example, in *The New Contented Little Baby Book* Gina Ford says five minutes each side every three hours is great:

> *The key to successful breastfeeding is getting off to the right start. All breastfeeding counsellors agree that in order to produce enough milk, it is essential that the breasts are stimulated frequently during the early days. I agree totally with this advice. Years ago, lack of breast stimulation was one of the main reasons breastfeeding failed when a strict four-hourly routine was adhered to ... I advise all my mothers to start off by offering five minutes each side every three hours, increasing the time by a few minutes each day until the milk comes in.*

In *Your Baby and Child* Penelope Leach, a more 'attachment'-based childcare theorist, says completely the opposite:

> *Nurse your baby as often as he is hungry. For the first week or so after your milk comes in that will probably be whenever he wakes up and may be as often as every hour, probably with a longer interval once or twice in the 24 hours. Certainly 12 to 15 feedings at this stage is not even unusual, much less undesirable. As long as you get the baby well latched on each time ... it does not matter how often you nurse him.*
>
> *Nurse your baby for as long as he likes. Traditional advice to limit sucking-time to two minutes (or five minutes) each side was bad advice that must have contributed to many 'nursing failures'.*

Richard Ferber, an American expert, and author of *Solving Your Child's Sleep Problems*, is scathing about 'demand feeding' (he is the 'sleep trainer' whose theory has led to the verb 'to Ferberize'):

> *Hourly feeding is exhausting for the mother, painful if you are breast-feeding, unnecessary for the baby, and interferes with his developing*

more normal and healthy sleep-wake and feeding patterns.

If your baby has been feeding every hour, begin to increase the time between feedings by an amount you feel comfortable with – perhaps 15 minutes per day – until he is being fed every two hours, then every two and a half or three hours.

In the end, the debate boils down to one between the child-centred, soft and fluffy attachment theorists, and the less soft and fluffy, more parent-centred 'common-sense' school that tends to favour routines. In this rather extreme example of the common-sense school, from *The Home Care of the Infant and Child*, published in 1931, Frederick Tisdall states, approvingly, that a well-trained baby is like a 'little machine':

'Regularity of nursing is most important. The infant should always be fed exactly at the stated hour and never at irregular intervals, as this upsets the baby's routine and soon leads to stomach trouble. If the infant wakes up and cries before the feeding hour he should be examined to see if he

is wet, and if so, changed and then
offered some plain boiled water.
If the infant is asleep
at the feeding hour he should be
awakened. It is remarkable how
these infants learn to wake up at or
shortly before the appointed time.
After a few days' training they behave
like little machines.'

~
Keep It Clean

The number of nursing-bottles from which to choose is very large indeed, and each one is said to have some special advantage possessed by no other … The best pattern is the so-called "Alexandra Feeding-bottle" with screw metal cap.

Perhaps I ought to explain why I think this is such an excellent bottle. It is because there is no porous material of any kind about it – no cork washer … however little cork there is about a feeding bottle, after a time it is sure to become saturated with the milk, and it is very difficult … to wash it out; it becomes sour, therefore, and is often the unexpected cause of the food also turning sour and disagreeing with the child.

Whatever kind of bottle, however, you may have or decide to get, it will be necessary to thoroughly cleanse it after each time of using it; let it be scalded with hot water – not only the bottle, but the glass and

India-rubber tubes, and the teat also. This cleanness is of the greatest advantage; nothing in fact tends to success in artificial feeding as attention to this point.

This advice from Thomas Bull's *Hints for Mothers* is advanced for the nineteenth century – it was the early twentieth century before people understood the nature of germs and that infection could be prevented by (for example) hand washing, and sterilising medical instruments with boiling water or antiseptic spray. However, the bottle he is recommending is the 'murder baby bottle' I mentioned earlier. The reason for its nickname is that the long tubes that attached its mouthpiece to the main body weren't transparent and it was impossible to clean them properly.

Weaning

When *Little Britain* did its breastfeeding sketch with David Walliams demanding 'bitty' (a conflation of 'breast' and 'titty' in case you're wondering) from his Home Counties mum, played by Geraldine James, a nation was plunged into the uncomfortable topic of late weaning. It may be helpful to remember that internationally the average age of weaning is four years, and the World Health Organization recommends it should be done at six months or older. However, Brits are not very comfortable with breastfeeding, and seem to want to get it over and done with as quickly as possible (statistically, the majority of breastfed infants in the United Kingdom are weaned onto solids by four months).

Looking at past pundits, this seems to have been the case for a long time. Thomas Bull is an example:

This [ill health while nursing] may arise out of one of two causes – either a parent continuing to suckle too long, or from not being equal to the continued drain on the system. Examples of the first class are met with daily. I refer to poor married women, who nurse their children eighteen months, two years or even longer than this, from the belief that by so doing they will prevent pregnancy. The consequences are a state of exhaustion and disorder of the general health, which often leads to most alarming maladies.

Bull thought too much nursing led to 'alarming maladies' for mum, while Mrs Beeton paints an even grimmer picture:

The length of time an infant should be suckled must depend much on the health and strength of the child, and the health of the mother, and the quantity and quality of her milk; though, when all circumstances are favourable, it should never be less than nine, nor exceed fifteen months; but perhaps the true time will be found in the medium between both. But of this we may be sure, that Nature never ordained a child to live on suction after having endowed it with teeth to bite and to grind; and nothing is more out of place and unseemly than to hear a child, with a set of twenty teeth, ask for 'the breast'.

Uh oh! 'Bitty'!

It worked for me

My whole life revolves around food. I am always trying out new things at work and at home. I breastfed Jack till he was about six months old. When it was time to go on to solid food I just gave him mushed-up versions of whatever I was cooking. It worked famously, perhaps because he got used to weird and wonderful tastes through the breast milk. He is now two and so far he will eat anything. So I think prepared baby food is a bit of a con. *Nicky, mother of Jack (2 years)*

'The practice of protracted wet-nursing is hurtful to the mother, by keeping up an uncalled-for, and, after the proper time, an unhealthy drain on her system, while the child either derives no benefit from what it no longer requires, or it produces a positive injury on its constitution. After the period when Nature has ordained the child shall live by other means, the secretion of milk becomes thin and deteriorated, showing in the flabby flesh and puny features of the child both its loss of nutritious properties and the want of more stimulating aliment.'

For Mrs Beeton, not only is protracted breastfeeding bad for mum, but it turns the baby into a 'flabby' yet 'puny' monster. Independence is what is needed for the busy Victorian mother:

'Though we have said that twelve months is about the medium time a baby should be suckled, we by no means wish to imply that a child should be fed exclusively on milk for its first year; quite the reverse; the infant can hardly be too soon made independent of the mother.'

There was lots of advice about which solid foods baby should be weaned on to. The 1878 edition of Chavasse's *Advice to a Mother* has pages on the subject. This is only a selection:

What food, when a babe is six or seven months old, is the best substitute for a mother's milk? The food that suits one infant will not agree with another. (1) The one that I have found the most generally useful, is made as follows – Boil the crumb of bread for two hours in water, taking particular care that it does not burn, then add only a little lump sugar (or brown sugar, if the bowels be costive), to make it palatable. When he is six or seven months old, mix a little new milk – the milk of ONE cow – with it gradually as he becomes older, increasing the quantity until it be nearly all milk, there being only enough water to boil the bread, the milk should be poured boiling hot on the bread. Sometimes the two milks – the mother's and the cow's milk – do not agree, when such is the case, let the milk be left out, both in this and in the foods following, and let the food be made with water, instead of with milk and water. In other respects, until the child is weaned, let it be made as above directed, when he is weaned, good fresh cow's milk MUST, as previously recommended, be used. (2) Or cut thin slices of bread into a basin, cover the bread with cold water, place it in an oven for two hours to bake, take it out, beat the bread up with a fork, and then slightly sweeten it.

During the eighteenth and nineteenth centuries the general consensus appears to have been that food for children should be bland and starchy, and that fresh fruit and vegetables frequently disagreed with them (some commentators think many children whose sore gums were thought to be the result of 'teething' were actually suffering from scurvy). The lack of fibre in their diet may also have led to constipation in many of them, which of course led to drastic treatments by anxious mums and doctors.

In Victorian times little was known about the foods that shouldn't be given to babies until they are six months old, such as salt and sugar, as well as eggs, full-fat cows' milk, nuts, shellfish, wheat and other allergens (Food Standards Authority guidelines). Most people thought sugar was nourishing and had few problems with salt. Cows' milk was often used as a substitute for breast milk, whereas nowadays we are told to avoid it during a baby's first year.

Mrs Beeton has a great deal of advice on foods for babies, both before and after weaning:

The articles generally employed as food for infants consist of arrowroot, bread, flour, baked flour, prepared groats, farinaceous food, biscuit-powder, biscuits, tops-and-bottoms, and semolina, or manna croup, as it is otherwise called, which, like tapioca, is the prepared pith of certain vegetable substances. Of this list the least efficacious, though, perhaps, the most believed in, is arrowroot, which only as a mere agent, for change, and then only for a very short time, should ever be employed as a means of diet to infancy or childhood. It is a thin, flatulent, and innutritious food, and incapable of supporting infantine life with energy. Bread, though the universal régime with the labouring poor, where the infant's stomach and digestive powers are a reflex, in miniature, of the father's, should never be given to an infant under three months, and, even then, however finely beaten up and smoothly made, is a very questionable diet.

Flour, when well boiled, though infinitely better than arrowroot, is still only a kind of fermentative paste, that counteracts its own good by after-acidity and flatulence.

As you can see, the Victorian baby had to be starch friendly. A recipe for tapioca soup was recommended by Mrs Beeton as being especially good for babies being weaned:

TAPIOCA SOUP

Ingredients – 5 oz. of tapioca, 2 quarts of stock No. 105 or 106.

Mode – Put the tapioca into cold stock, and bring it gradually to a boil. Simmer gently till tender, and serve.

Time – Rather more than 1 hour. Average cost. 1s. or 6d. per quart.

Seasonable all the year.

Sufficient for 8 persons.

TAPIOCA.–This excellent farinaceous food is the produce of the pith of the cassava-tree, and is made in the East Indies, and also in Brazil. It is, by washing, procured as a starch from the tree, then dried, either in the sun or on plates of hot iron, and afterwards broken into grains, in which form it is imported into this country. Its nutritive properties are large, and as a food for persons of delicate digestion, or for children, it is in great estimation. 'No amylaceous substance,' says Dr. Christison, 'is so much relished by infants about the time of weaning; and in them it is less apt to become sour during digestion than any other farinaceous food, even arrowroot not excepted.'

My favourite baby-weaning food advice is in Truby King's *Feeding and Care of Baby*:

'GIVE BABY A BONE
At six months of age a chicken-bone
or chop-bone (from which all
but a trace of meat has been
removed) may be given to baby at
mealtimes, as the munching of this
tends to promote a free flow of blood
to the developing teeth.'

~
Teething

In a letter to her faithless first lover, Mary Wollstonecraft talks about their daughter's teething pangs:

[PARIS, 1795]

> *My animal is well; I have not yet taught her to eat, but nature is doing the business. I gave her a crust to assist the cutting of her teeth; and now she has two, she makes good use of them to gnaw a crust, biscuit, etc. You would laugh to see her; she is just like a little squirrel; she will guard a crust for two hours; and, after, fixing her eye on an object for some time, dart on it with an aim as sure as a bird of prey – nothing can equal her life and spirits. I suffer from a cold; but it does not affect her.*

Mrs Beeton recognised that teething was unpleasant, but counsels against sleeping draughts (opiates and other dangerous sleeping potions that nurses and mothers frequently gave to babies):

> *Dentition is usually the first serious trouble, bringing many other disorders in its train. The symptoms are most perceptible to the mother: the child sucks feebly, and with gums hot, inflamed, and swollen. In this case, relief is yielded by rubbing them from time to time with a little of Mrs. Johnson's soothing syrup, a valuable and perfectly safe medicine. Selfish and thoughtless nurses, and mothers too, sometimes give cordials and sleeping-draughts, whose effects are too well known.*

Many doctors treated sore gums by 'lancing' – cutting teeth out of the gums. Because of the poor hygiene of the day, children were often killed by this.

However, at least nineteenth-century pundits didn't tell breastfeeding mothers they couldn't take a biting baby off the nipple, as some twentieth-century ones did, telling unfortunate mums their babies would suffer from rejection anxiety if they said 'No'. Penelope Leach is more reasonable:

> *Try to say 'No' very firmly and calmly; slip your finger into his mouth to take him off the nipple, and end the feeding for now.*

Solid Foods

> *Take a pound of lean beef, free from fat and separated from the bones, chop it up as mince-meat; pour upon it a pint of cold water, let it stand for two or three hours, and then slowly heat to boiling; and, after boiling briskly for a minute or two, strain the liquid through a fine sieve or cloth, and add a sufficiency of salt. The same plan may be adopted with mutton, veal, or chicken.*

As the child advances in age [a month or so after the large molars appear] … a portion, now and then, of a soft boiled egg may be given; and by-and-by a small bread-pudding, made with one egg in it, may form the dinner meal. Nothing is more common than for parents, during this period, to give their children solid animal food. This is a great and mischievous error.

As this quote from Thomas Bull's *Hints for Mothers* suggests, in the eighteenth and nineteenth centuries solid foods tended to be very much on the floury, starchy or meaty side. Most writers thought vegetables and fruit produced wind, and wouldn't have countenanced our five-a-day regimen.

Things had improved by Truby King's day. He disapproved of starchy 'mush' as well as rusks and biscuits, and emphasised the importance of 'self-cleaning' foods like apples (all to be given to babies at nine months). Photographs in *Feeding and Care of Baby* compare healthy Maori teeth to 'degenerate' European ones. Vegetables began to make a welcome appearance in the weaned baby's diet:

VEGETABLE PUREE
Use vegetables such as carrot, cauliflower, turnip. Steam or simmer gently until tender. Add pinch of salt. Mash through sieve.
    Note – cook all vegetables in very little water and for no longer than is required to make them tender. Save the water they are cooked in for making broths and gravy. (It contains valuable mineral elements out of the vegetables; children need these.)

However, it was not until the 1950s that books like Ursula James's *Feeding in Infancy and Early Childhood* included information about nutrients like vitamins. She gives detailed instructions for weaning foods (as well as gasp-inducing menus for older children including sardines on toast and offal such as tripe – I wish my children were so adventurous).

5–6 MONTHS

8.30 am Fruit juice on waking
Egg with bread and butter
Cup of milk

1 pm Vegetables with minced meat or fish
Milk pudding, custard or junket
Fruit
Orange juice and water

4 pm Cereal and fruit
Plain cake, rusks, or bread and butter with
honey, syrup or Marmite, or cheese
Cup of milk

6.30 pm Milk feed
(during this period
breastfeeding will
gradually be given up)

This menu has a reassuring,
timeless sound about it; a kind
of pipe-and-slippers baby
menu. Today ideas about what
is suitable for an older baby
and what isn't can be
confusing, as Penelope
Leach states:

'Ideas of which particular food are suitable or unsuitable for an older baby vary dramatically from country to country and have far more to do with convention than diet. There are very few foods which you eat but which your baby should not have. As long as you avoid much salt, extra sugar, hot spices, alcohol, coffee or tea, he can try anything you are cooking.'

Apart from the foods listed below by the Netmums weaning guide for 6–12 months, that is – although it's questionable how many parents in the United Kingdom are feeding their children shark:

Honey
Salt
Shark, swordfish or marlin (due to high mercury levels)
Goats and sheep's milk
Mould-ripened soft cheeses

And what about organic food? Penelope Leach, for example, tells us to 'Buy organic babyfoods … buy organic fruit and vegetables when you can'. Many of us will obey this diktat. But what about Christopher Green's description of a perfect menu in *Toddler Taming*:

> *In one morning you can cook carrots, cauliflower, pumpkin, steak, chicken, fish and apples, pop them in the liquidiser (one at a time), and then put them into individual ice-cube trays for freezing. When mealtime comes, all you have to do is look in the freezer and decide on the menu, defrost it, and there you have a small portion of an instant but fresh-made meal. This idea can be carried through to toddlerhood as well, using slightly larger containers and of course non liquidised food.*

Phew! What a busy morning, especially if you're looking after baby as well … Charlotte Raven in the *Guardian* makes an amusing case for trying to avoid menu-planning control freakery, as a toddler will always have its own ideas about what it will and won't eat:

> *Our weekly menu planner indicated sole in creamy mushroom sauce, followed by a choice of home-made frozen yoghurt or peaches with amaretti biscuits. I set about it, ignoring her cries for attention.*
>
> *'Look, Baby,' I said with some pride. 'A beautifully cooked and presented meal of locally sourced fish with porcini. Mmmmm.' 'Get down, Mummy,' she said, after two mouthfuls. I put her on the floor and started clearing up.*
>
> *'Mummy?' She tugged at my skirt with the clear intention of dragging me down to her level.*
>
> *'Leave me alone a minute darling.' Irritated, I reached for the Hemp Seed Bar.*
>
> *''Anna's!' She held up her arms imploringly.*
>
> *'Go on then,' I said, 'Just a bite.' She seized it and rammed the whole bar, plastic wrapper and all, down her throat.*
>
> *'Charlotte's!' something inside me protested. 'Charlotte's treat!'*

'Give it back!' I lunged for it but she was too quick.
'NO!' she screamed
I was indignant. 'Baby Anna, surely you know that you are meant to share.' I snatched it away, oblivious to her cries.
(15 JULY 2006)

Every mother, however loving, will have days when her patience wears thin. For these moments I recommend 'The Duchess's Lullaby' from Lewis Carroll's *Alice in Wonderland,* which is a wonderful antidote to all those frozen cubes of organic baby food.

The Duchess's Lullaby

Speak roughly to your little boy,
And beat him when he sneezes;
He only does it to annoy,
Because he knows it teases.

Wow! wow! wow!

I speak severely to my boy,
And beat him when he sneezes:
For he can thoroughly enjoy
The pepper when he pleases!

Wow! wow! wow!

LEWIS CARROLL

sleep!

crying
gurgling

And So To Bed

Rock a bye baby on the tree top,
When the wind blows the cradle will rock,
When the bough breaks the cradle will fall,
And down will come baby, cradle and all.

The other day I was singing 'Rock a Bye Baby' to my younger daughter, Lydia, when my older daughter, Ottilie, remarked, 'It's not a very nice song, is it?'. This drove me to the Internet to find out more about it. According to the *Great American Baby Almanac* one of the Pilgrim Fathers, who arrived in America in the *Mayflower* in 1620, was inspired to write it when he saw the Wampanoag native peoples hanging their cradleboards in trees during fine weather (cradleboards are traditional and sometimes still used today).

Somehow, 'Rock a Bye Baby' reflects the feeling of despair parents experience when they try to get their babies to sleep. There was obvious concern about the latent violence in the song, and later versions have extra verses of a soppier kind:

> *Baby is drowsing*
> *Cosy and fair*
> *Mother sits near*
> *In her rocking chair*
> *Forward and back*
> *The cradle she swings*
> *And though baby sleeps*
> *He hears what she sings*
>
> *From the high rooftops*
> *Down to the sea*
> *No one's as dear*
> *As baby to me*
> *Wee little fingers*
> *Eyes wide and bright*
> *Now sound asleep*
> *Until morning light*

If you are worried about traumatising your newborn, you can always add these to the original song!

Seriously though, sleeping is probably the biggest issue for new parents. Those well-meant questions such as 'Is she sleeping through the night yet?' when you are still at the stage where night and day seem to merge into one sleepless blur can hit home hard. Most adults don't know what sleep deprivation is like until they experience it, and it can come as a dreadful shock. On the other hand, some babies seem to emerge from the womb knowing how to fit in and sleep through the night from day one. My first child did this from about eight weeks. I can't say it had anything to do with my superior child-rearing, I think she just got into the habit. But at the time I thought I had it sussed – so imagine my horror when baby number two comes along and doesn't sleep through the night successfully until she starts nursery school. Nature or nurture? The childcare experts keep themselves in designer handbags by convincing desperate parents that a particular sleep routine will unlock the key to an uninterrupted night's sleep, but I think a lot of luck is involved. Try all the methods on offer by all means, but remember that however bad things are, having a teenager (and believe me you will one day) who never stops sleeping is worse.

Baby It's Cold Outside

First of all, there's the question of where the baby should sleep. In the eighteenth century, it was seen as natural for babies to be in the same bed as their mother or nurse. It kept the child warm and contented in cold houses, although there was anxiety, as there is today, over 'overlaying' (suffocation). Even in the mid-nineteenth century, Victorian commentators allowed a baby to sleep with its nurse or mother, at least for the first few months of its life: 'The bosom of the mother is the natural pillow of her offspring' was the opinion of a Dr Conquest in his *Letters to a Mother*.

By the late nineteenth century, baby was firmly in the nursery. This was made easier by the use of a cot, or sometimes a cradle.

The twentieth-century expectation was definitely that a baby would have its own room, although the caveat was often that it might sleep in its parents' one for the first six months. This is Dr Spock's advice in the 1957 edition of *Baby and Child Care*:

It is preferable to get your baby used to the idea that he always goes to bed and to sleep right after a meal. (An occasional baby won't fall easily into this pattern but insists on being sociable after his meals. I'd try to change his mind). It is good, too, for him to get used to falling asleep in his own bed, without company, at least by the time any 3 month colic is over ... Out of the parents' room by six months if possible. A child can sleep in a room by himself from the time he is born, if convenient, as long as the parents are near enough to hear him when he cries. Better not let the child in your bed ... [the child] is apt to cling to the security of his parents' bed, and there is the devil to pay getting him out again.

Three-in-a-bed Shock

In the last ten years or so co-sleeping has come out of the closet. The invention of clever devices that make it safer for parents to sleep with their children in or near their beds (the American 'Snugglenest', or cots with let-down sides or an extension that slides under the parents' mattress, are examples) means they can sleep with their baby without worrying about rolling over on it in the night. A recent kerfuffle in the world of childcare theory occurred when Richard Ferber (the 'sleep trainer') mentioned that he no longer thought it was tantamount to child abuse to let children sleep in their parents' beds. A lot of co-sleeping parents 'came out' once their practice was sanctioned by the American guru, who was apparently rather bemused by the excited reaction to his opinion. Meanwhile, the idea now has enthusiastic supporters, such as Deborah Jackson (who says it makes for an easier relationship) and Margot Sunderland (who claims that separation from their parents at bedtime makes cortisol levels rise in babies and toddlers).

Here is Margot Sunderland, author of *The Science of Parenting*, on co-sleeping, in an interview with the *Sunday Times* in 2006:

> *There is a taboo in this country about children sleeping with their parents ... What I have done in this book is present the science. Studies from around the world show that co-sleeping until the age of five is an investment for the child. They can have separation anxiety up to the age of five and beyond, which can affect them in later life. This is calmed by co-sleeping.*

But for every co-sleeping devotee there is a childcare 'expert', usually an ex-maternity nurse, who thinks it is the devil's work. According to Gina Ford in *The New Contented Little Baby Book*, 'Bed sharing ... more often than not ends up with parents sleeping in separate rooms' and overtired mothers,

It worked for me

We have always slept with our kids. As more and more of them came along we just bought a bigger bed. As the children got older they naturally came to a point, usually aged five or six, when they wanted to have their own bed. It all worked perfectly for us. The only difficulty came from other people who found it rather threatening. But we stuck with it and now all the children sleep happily in their own beds, although they will still all get into our bed when there is a thunderstorm! *Daniel, father of four* a situation that 'puts enormous pressure on the family as a whole'. She thinks parents should establish sleep routines for very young babies, in separate rooms away from the rest of the house, and insists they teach them to sleep without the assistance of adults:

'All too often a mother will ring me up in a complete panic asking for advice on how to get a three-month-baby used to their own room. Many tears and much anxiety could have been avoided if the mother had got the baby used to his own room from day one ... When my babies are very small, if they have become over-tired or overstimulated, I find that they will calm down immediately when taken to their room. And by six weeks they are positively beaming when taken to their nursery for the bath and bedtime routine.'

crying
gurgling

baby

So, whether you are reading this book tucked up with your baby or luxuriating in your own personal space, there is an expert out there to make you feel you have made the right choice.

Cot Death

Meanwhile, the debate about Sudden Infant Death Syndrome continues to rage. Is it more likely when co-sleeping, because of the risks of unsafe bedding and overheating? Or less likely, as some co-sleeping advocates have it, because it helps babies adjust their breathing and regulate their temperature? (Studies show that the rate of cot deaths is very low in countries like Japan, where babies regularly sleep with their mother, but genetic factors may also be at work.)

It's worth remembering that until very recently the advice was to put babies on their stomachs to sleep, to avoid the risk of choking on vomit (Spock advocated this in 1957, for example) while recent research has confirmed without any doubt that they sleep most safely on their backs. In other words, it takes a while for advice to catch up with science, and science is not infallible either.

Cots and Cradles

It was the Greek physician Galen (AD 129–99) who first observed that the best ways to soothe a baby are to sing to it, rock it in a cradle or suckle it (or at least he was the first to write the information down; I'm sure mothers knew this earlier, or the human race might never have survived). Cradles that allow a rocking motion have existed for centuries; some of the earliest were hollowed-out tree trunks or rushwork baskets.

Even in today's paranoid times there isn't an anti-baby-rocking lobby, but in the eighteenth century rocking your baby was as controversial as co-sleeping is now. Some critics thought it was useful mainly for servants who didn't want to pay attention to their charges and found it easier to rock them; others, like Jean Jacques Rousseau, felt it was simply unnatural:

It is never necessary and often harmful to rock children in the cradle.

Cradles went in and out of fashion, and remained controversial during the nineteenth century. Perhaps this was due to some overenthusiastic (or even cruel) rocking. This is what Thomas Bull has to say in *Hints to Mothers*:

> *Gentle and cautious tossing, or rather dandling to and fro, is really agreeable to a child, and can never, therefore, be objectionable; but the rough treatment alluded to [violent jolting] a mother must carefully prevent. The same precaution it is necessary to observe in regard to the rocking an infant in a cradle. I believe that gentle and cautious rocking is a soothing and useful exercise to a child; but it is quite otherwise when rough and long-continued.*

A cot, a miniature bed, was preferred to a cradle. By the end of the nineteenth century, it was usually made of metal, which was seen to be more hygienic, and was less prone to damp. Some cots had a kind of valance or curtain to protect the baby from draughts. The nineteenth-century baby expert Chavasse, author of *Advice to a Mother*, disapproved of these:

> *If the head of the crib be covered, the babe cannot breathe freely, the air within the crib becomes contaminated, and thus the lungs cannot properly perform their functions. If his sleep is to be refreshing, he must breathe pure air. I do not even approve of a head to a crib. A child is frequently allowed to sleep on a bed with the curtains drawn completely close, as though it were dangerous for a breath of air to*

blow upon him [I have somewhere read that if a cage containing a canary be suspended at night within a bed where a person is sleeping, and the curtains be drawn closely around, that the bird will, in the morning, in all probability, be found dead!] This practice is most injurious. An infant must have the full benefit of the air of the room; indeed, the bed room door ought to be frequently left ajar, so that the air of the apartment may be changed, taking care, of course, not to expose him to a draught. If the flies, while he is asleep, annoy him, let a net veil be thrown over his face, as he can readily breathe through net, but not through a handkerchief.

By the twentieth century the idea that if the rocking motion was soothing to babies it wasn't necessarily a bad thing was becoming acceptable again. As commentators recognised, it reminds a baby of being in the womb or in its mother's arms.

Jean Liedloff, the author of *The Continuum Concept*, the earth mother's bible, believes that a human baby naturally behaves a lot like an animal one, clinging to its mother as she moves about (the 'in arms' concept). This means it hates prams, beds (apart from the parents' bed) and playpens (although surely it approves of slings?):

What he [the human baby] is not prepared for is a greater leap of any sort, let alone a leap into nothingness, non-life, a basket with dead cloth in it, or a plastic box without motion, sound, odor or the feel of life. The violent tearing apart of the mother-child continuum, so strongly established during the phases which took part in the womb, may understandably result in depression for the mother, as well as agony for the infant.

Every nerve ending under his newly exposed skin craves the expected embrace, all his being, the character of all he is, leads to his being held in arms ...

However, Liedloff recognises that the sensation of rocking is soothing for babies, although she disapproves of creating it by artificial means:

The carriage is jiggled by his mother who has learned that this tends to keep him quiet. The aching want of motion, an experience that all his antecedents had in their first months, is slightly lessened by the jiggling which, in its meagre way, gives him some experience rather than none ... carriage jiggling and cradles that rock offer another approximation. But the motion is so poor and clumsy a substitute for that in arms, that it does little to still the longings of the isolated infant.

I hate to think what she would have to say about modern mechanical rocking chairs for babies.

There's a great scene in *Sex and the City* where Miranda's son, Brady, won't stop crying until a sympathetic neighbour gives her a mechanical rocking chair. However, the chair breaks when Samantha is baby-sitting to allow Miranda to get a much-needed haircut. Unfazed, Samantha sticks her new vibrator under the chair to keep him quiet. And it works!

Most modern parents spend a lot of time driving their babies around in car seats (instant sleep guaranteed, unless you're on a long car journey), pushing them in prams or 'walking the floor' either to soothe them or put them to sleep. I've also heard tales of parents putting the baby's basket on top of a washing machine, although perhaps this was before the days of the bouncy chair ...

The Nursery

Childcare experts through the ages have always enjoyed laying down the law about where children should be housed. This is Leslie George Houden, OBE, MD, adviser in parentcraft to the Ministry of Health in 1958, apparently a lifelong member of the British Eugenics Society, and author of *The Art of Mothercraft*, on the subject of nurseries before the Second World War:

> *The nursery of many children is also the kitchen, the dining room and the sitting room, while in some parts of Ireland, it is a lounge for the family pigs and chicken as well. At the other end of the scale are the children who possess a suite of rooms of their own. In all cases, the principles governing the planning of a healthy nursery are the same … We will suppose we are to have both a day-nursery and a night-nursery … The night-nursery should also face south, with windows facing two ways, to avoid rain and droughts. Plain, clean-looking furniture, easily washed paint, a fitted carpet and a warm rug in front of the fire, make a cosy room. This fire will probably be either a gas or an electric one, as it is not needed during the day and open fires make so much extra work. The furniture will depend on the age of the child or children. When the baby is quite young, it is wiser for his nurse to sleep in the same room. Part of the earliest training of a baby is to persuade him to go through the night without having a wet bed … Every baby should have his own cot from the very first. He should never sleep in his mother's bed.*

The layout of a nursery hasn't varied much over the years. Victorian nurseries were very similar to the one described above (although gas fires and stoves went in and out of fashion in the nineteenth century, partly because nurses were suspected of sending recalcitrant children to sleep by gassing them). Here is Mrs Beeton's advice in her *Book of Household Management*:

In all cases, cleanliness, fresh air, clean utensils, and frequent washing of the person, both of nurse and children, are even more necessary in the nursery than in either drawing-room or sick-room, inasmuch as the delicate organs of childhood are more susceptible of injury from smells and vapours than adults.

Quite a few Victorian and Edwardian baby experts were bent on improving the race, hence the talk about 'sturdy' as opposed to 'puny' or 'degenerate' babies and so on. There was also a concern with class differences. Were working-class babies somehow sturdier (and thus, perhaps, threatening a takeover)? Were upper-class women too 'feminine' to bear and nurse children successfully (meaning, were the upper classes literally a dying breed)? The suspicion is that there was a hidden agenda – that many manuals were lierally 'training' an elite cadre of healthy, independent, cold-bath-loving Empire-builders. This is Chavasse, in *Advice to a Mother*:

The nursery ought to be the largest and the most airy room in the house. In the town, if it be in the topmost story (provided the apartment be large and airy) so much the better, as the air will then be purer. The architect, in the building of a house, ought to be particularly directed to pay attention to the space, the loftiness, the ventilation, the light, the warming, and the conveniences of a nursery. A bath-room attached to it will be of great importance and benefit to the health of a child.

It will be advantageous to have a water-closet near at hand, which should be well supplied with water, be well drained, and be well ventilated. If this be not practicable, the evacuations ought to be removed as soon as they are passed. It is a filthy and an idle habit of a nurse-maid to allow a motion to remain for any length of time in the room.

Filthy and idle! It's hard to know what Chavasse would have made of modern nappy-bins (not to mention that peculiar artefact, the perfumed nappy bag). He also emphasises the importance of fresh air (see opposite).

'The VENTILATION of a nursery is of paramount importance. There ought to be a constant supply of fresh pure air in the apartment. But how few nurseries have fresh, pure air! Many nurseries are nearly hermetically sealed — the windows are seldom, if ever, opened; the doors are religiously closed; and, in summer time, the chimneys are carefully stuffed up, so that a breath of air is not allowed to enter! The consequences are, the poor unfortunate children "are poisoned by their own breaths", and are made so delicate that they are constantly catching cold; indeed, it might be said that they are labouring under chronic catarrhs, all arising from Nature's laws being set at defiance.'

~
Putting Colour in Baby's Cheeks

Victorians were very exercised about fresh air. Babies might be carried under open windows or taken outside for 'sun baths' in summer and exercise in winter. They were seen as being similar to little plants in their need for sun and air. Interestingly, this still applies in some northern European countries. I saw an Internet forum recently where a Finnish mother discussed putting her baby to sleep outside when the temperature was 'only minus 15° Centigrade'. Apparently babies sleep better outside and it's good for colds. A 'simple hat' was all that was necessary for the child's head, in what the mother described as 'this stupid summer weather we have nowadays'.

Fresh air was even more of an obsession in the twentieth century than it was in the nineteenth. Dr Spock's mother, Mildred, was an aficionado of Dr Luther Emmett Holt, the author of *Feeding and Care of Baby*, a popular child-care manual in the United States. In *Dr Spock: An American Life* Thomas Maier describes how she made all her children sleep on the porch of their Connecticut home, whatever the weather, and sent them to an outdoor school:

> *'For my mother, fresh air was of enormous importance,' Benjamin Spock recalls of those winter nights in 1910. Fresh air was pure and chaste and wholesome, just as Mildred Spock determined her children would be. 'You didn't rebel against fresh air,' recalls her oldest son, 'because fresh air was just as sacred as morality.'*
>
> *The sleeping porch rested on the second floor of the Spocks' Victorian home, above the front-door veranda with its white picket railing. A large, striped canvas hanging over the sleeping porch from a metal awning kept away the rain and snow. Sometimes gusts of wind off the Long Island Sound howled memorably. When rain came, the water trickled down the canvas flaps. In the darkness, the sleeping porch became its own world. 'The streetlamps would light up these little drops and we thought*

they were fairies running along,' remembers Ben's sister, Marjorie, who everyone called Hiddy. 'There was a certain magic out there.'

It's a touching scene: the frozen little Spocks huddling together picturing fairies running along the porch. Tellingly, when he was talking about the way he responded to criticism by feminists, Spock mentioned that from his childhood he had 'been used to being criticised'. And he was the favourite child! No wonder *Baby and Child Care* is so famously unjudgemental.

In the final version of the book, he kept the reference to fresh air in the main text but removed it from the index … perhaps a dig at his mother? This is what he had to say about it in 1957:

> *Fresh air. Changes of air temperature are beneficial in toning up the body's system for adapting to cold or heat … Cool or cold air improves appetite, puts color in the cheeks, and gives more pep to humans of all ages. A baby living continuously in a warm room usually has a pasty complexion and may have a sluggish appetite … it's good for a baby (like anyone else) to get outside for 2 or 3 hours a day.*

In Scandinavian countries it is common practice to have outdoor kindergartens even in the depths of winter. Educational theorists believe the children learn faster and lose fewer days to illness.

~ No More Nurseries

Some attachment-parenting theorists nowadays want to do away with the nursery altogether. Deborah Jackson, author of *Three in a Bed*, is an example:

> *When we don't know what to do with our babies, at least there are a hundred products to explore. And that is what makes it so hard for us to discard the cot. To do without a crib or a cradle is to deprive the nursery of its advertised centrepiece.*

We are encouraged to picture our babies lying in their own rooms at night, surrounded by fluffy bunnies and pastel-coloured alphabets. To deny this image is to destroy the whole vision of motherhood for many women in the West. Decking out a nursery is as important as choosing a white wedding dress. Our culture endorses the ritual of the nursery. And if you have a nursery and a cot, you have to have bedtimes and rules, battles and broken hearts.

~ Sleep Routines – Bed by the Book

> *People who say they sleep like a baby usually don't have one.*
> LEO J. BURKE

Trying to get a baby to sleep at the right time is not a new problem (although there are new grandmothers who like to suggest they had no such difficulties when their children were young). Advice, like Chavasse's, on getting your child into a sleep routine has been dispensed since Victorian times:

Do you recommend a child, in the middle of the day, to be put to sleep?

Let him be put on his mattress awake, that he may sleep for a couple of hours before dinner [Chavasse is referring to the midday meal, presumably the baby 'supped' at supper time], then he will rise both refreshed and strengthened for the remainder of the day. I said, let him be put down awake. He might, for the first few times, cry, but, by perseverance, he will without any difficulty fall to sleep. The practice of sleeping before dinner ought to be continued until he be three years old, and, if he can be prevailed upon, even longer. For if he do not have sleep in the middle of the day, he will all the afternoon and the evening be cross; and when he does go to bed, he will probably be too tired to sleep, or, his nerves having been exhausted by the long wakefulness, he will fall into a troubled, broken slumber, and not into that sweet, soft, gentle repose, so characteristic of healthy, happy childhood!

In the early twentieth century, followers of the New Zealand baby expert Sir Frederick Truby King didn't only specify when a baby should sleep, they also laid down rules for how long the sleep should last. This extract from Mabel Liddiard's *The Mothercraft Manual,* first published in 1923, is an example:

Sleep. The baby doubles his weight in the first six months of life, therefore needs a great deal of sleep, during which Nature repairs waste and attends to the growth of the whole organism. For the first month an infant should sleep all the time except while being fed and dressed. As he grows older he needs to be awake part of the day; it is best to train him to sleep in the morning and to be awake in the afternoon. The consecutive hours of sleep during the night are of the utmost importance, hence the wrong of beginning the habit of night feeds and disturbed nights. The infant should be put to bed in a well-ventilated room by himself from the earliest days after the 6pm feed, until a year old, wakened carefully in a dimly-lighted room for the 10pm feed and later held out in the dark at this time, if possible.

Note the magisterial tone: Mabel Liddiard clearly had no truck with disobedient babies or sloppy mums. 'Holding out' means being put on the potty, even as a newborn, of which more later. She quotes Truby King's table of averages for sleeping and waking:

Age	Hours needed to sleep	Hours awake
1 month	21	3
6 months	18	6
1 year	15	9

These figures are surprising to modern parents. In *The New Contented Little Baby Book,* published in 2002, Gina Ford describes her ideal sleep routine:

> *By three to four months most babies are capable of sleeping 12 hours at night, provided their daytime sleep is no more than three to three and a half hours, divided between two or three naps a day. If you want your baby to sleep from 7/7.30pm to 7/7.30am, it is very important that you structure these naps so that he has his longest nap at midday, with two shorter ones – one in the morning and one late afternoon.*

So Gina Ford is suggesting 15 or 15 ½ hours' sleep a day as an ideal for a baby at three or four months. A Truby King mother would probably have aimed at two and a half to three more hours for a baby of that age, and would probably have obediently ignored it if it was trying to attract her attention. No wonder Truby King babies were independent … For comparison, here is a modern sleep chart from the US Pampers website article 'Your Baby's Sleep Patterns'.

Age	Approx. amount of sleep needed
Newborn	16 to 20 hours each
4 months	9 to 12 hours plus two naps (2 to 3 hours each)
6 months	11 hours plus two naps (1 ½ to 2 ½ hours each)
9 months	11 to 12 hours plus two naps (1 to 2 hours each)
1 year	10 to 11 hours plus two naps (1 to 2 hours each)

Could there be something in the assertion that children sleep less than they used to? These are some of the results of a survey of 2000 new parents and 2000 people aged 55 to 65 carried out by *Mother and Baby* and *Yours* magazines:

> *[It found] today's parents try all kinds of things to get their babies to sleep through the night, including taking the infant into their own bed.*
>
> *In contrast, parents in the 1960s and 1970s tended to say their babies had slept peacefully in their own cots.*
>
> *New mothers of young babies reported that, on average, they only have three and a half hours sleep a night, compared to five hours which the older generation said they used to get.*
>
> *Two thirds of those surveyed said this 'sleep starvation' left them feeling bad-tempered, with the same proportion reporting irritation with their partner.*
>
> *Six out of 10 say lack of sleep has 'spoilt their sex-life' and 84% say they 'prefer sleep to sex'.*
>
> *But the survey found only around a third of women who had been mothers in the 1960s and 1970s, when most did not work, ever felt bad-tempered or irritable with their partner due to lack of sleep – and only 12% said lack of sleep spoilt their sex life.*

It's hard to know what to conclude from these statistics: either babies are sleeping less, or our mothers and grandmothers have forgotten the bad bits!

Victorians like Chavasse also had clear ideas about sleeping times:

'At what hour ought a child to be put to bed in the evening? At six in the winter, and at seven o'clock in the summer. Regularity ought to be observed, as regularity is very conducive to health. It is a reprehensible practice to keep a child up until nine or ten o'clock at night. If this be done, he will, before his time, become old, and the seeds of disease will be sown.'

As did Truby King in *Feeding and Care of Baby*:

> *Children should be put to bed regularly at a reasonable hour. It is well to continue the morning sleep or rest until the child is five or six years old, especially during the summer, when children wake early. This can easily be accomplished if there is a little firmness on the mother's part. A short sleep or rest restores a child wonderfully, and the result is that there is no crossness or fatigue at the end of the day.*

In contrast, Jean Liedloff describes a typical bedtime for a baby from the Yequana tribe, who is 'in arms' until he can walk unaided:

> *If there is a party while he is asleep, he will be jounced quite violently while his mother hops and stamps in time to the music. Through daytime sleep, similar adventures befall him. At night, his mother sleeps beside him, her skin next to his, as always, while she breathes and moves and sometimes snores a little. She wakens often during the night to tend the*

fire, holding him close as she rolls out of her hammock and slips to the floor where he is sandwiched between her thigh and body as she rearranges the logs. If he awakens hungry in the night he may cry if he cannot find her breast; she will then give it to him and again his well-being will be re-established, without ever having come near to straining the limits of his continuum [his evolutionary expectations of constant contact].

Perhaps this is the moment to mention the bedtime tactics of Laura Ashley, the textile and home-furnishings queen. When her four children were small she was so desperate to have time to get on with her designing that she put all the clocks in the house forward by two hours so that she could say she was putting them to bed at seven when it was really five o'clock.

It worked for me

Tim and Emma's first child had colic and cried constantly between about 6 p.m. and 9 p.m. every night. Trying to deal with her was 'unrelenting, unrewarding. She was unhappy and being cuddled wouldn't soothe her. It was very stressful.' They started using Gina Ford's sleep-training techniques.

'It was amazing. We did the routine. You have to teach them how to fall asleep on their own. Previously, she'd gone to sleep "on us" and then had to be put down. Controlled crying doesn't work if you haven't followed the sleep and feeding routine during the day. Babies need to have a big feed, and then they go to sleep. It took two days to sleep train Grace, twenty minutes on the first day and five minutes on the second day. We had no more disturbed nights until she was three. It's a cliché, but she transformed. She went from being an angry little baby – put on weight, and transformed.'

They faced some hostility over their choice of guru, however. 'We went out to a dinner party, and our baby was asleep in a spare room while another couple were still struggling with theirs at 9 p.m. We commented that Grace was "Gina'd" and we no longer had any trouble with her at night. The other couple walked out!' *Tim and Emma, parents of Grace (5 years) and Frank (1 year)*

~
Crybaby Bunting: Colic

Colic is the common diagnosis for healthy babies who cry inconsolably, usually for up to three hours in the evening, from about the first three weeks to the first three months of their lives. Today we're usually told it's nothing to do with their digestion but is more of a developmental issue, although wind can make it worse. Historically, though, colic was seen as a digestive problem because babies with colic frequently draw their legs up to their stomach.

Here is Chavasse on the subject:

> *In pain either of the stomach or of the bowels, there is nothing usually affords greater or speedier relief than the external application of heat. The following are four different methods of applying heat:– 1. A bag of hot salt – that is to say, powdered table-salt – put either into the oven or into a frying-pan over the fire, and thus made hot, and placed in a flannel bag … 2. An india rubber hot-water bottle, half filled with hot water – it need not be boiling – applied to the stomach or to the bowels, will afford great comfort. Another and an excellent remedy for these cases is a hot bran poultice … 4. In case a child has a feverish cold, especially if it be attended, as it sometimes is, with pains in the*

It worked for me

My baby Nat had the most terrible colic. He cried day and night for what seemed like months. I hated the idea that I could nothing to comfort him. The only thing that would quieten him down was carrying him with my arm underneath his tummy. Maybe the warmth or the pressure was soothing. *Clare, mother of Nat* (**3 years**) *bowels, the following is a good external application.— Take a yard of flannel, fold it in three widths, then dip it in very hot water, wring it out tolerably dry, and apply it evenly and neatly round and round the bowels; over this, and to keep it in its place, and to keep in the moisture, put on a dry flannel bandage, four yards long and four inches wide ... Either the one or the other, then, of the above applications will usually, in pains of the stomach and bowels, afford great relief.*

Mabel Liddiard, in the 1920s, agreed with Chavasse:

Colic. Severe pain in the stomach or abdomen may be due to wrong food, overfeeding, too frequent feeding, cold food, food taken too quickly or too slowly, diarrhoea or constipation. If the child has definite pain he will scream and draw up his legs and will continue to cry even when being nursed.

Treatment. Remedy any of the above causes; for local treatment if the immediate cause is wind in the stomach, give a teaspoonful of dill water in two teaspoons of warm, boiled water, or a pinch of soda bicarbonate in warm water. Hold the baby over the shoulder, gently patting his back; this should help bring up the wind. Warmth applied to the abdomen often affords relief; care must be taken not to burn the infant.

It worked for me

Once you settle into the fussy evenings they are not too bad. I found it took about five weeks of bad colic to break my resistance to the idea [Mary-Anne didn't want to supplement with formula, which she thinks could ease colic but at the risk of allergies]. After that it seemed normal and even fairly simple to manage. It lasted quite a long time – about six months altogether, although the last two were quite a lot better. *Mary-Anne, mother of Lisa (2 ¾ years)*

Truby King's cure for a severe attack of colic is the most drastic – I wouldn't like to try to give an enema to a screaming baby:

An enema given at 100 deg. F. and hot flannel wrappings applied at the same time to the abdomen afford the best means of treating a severe attack of colic. Not only is the pain relieved, but for the time being the cause is removed by the evacuation of wind and irritating material.

The Well-dressed Baby: Nightwear

Up to the early eighteenth century swaddling was used to subdue and pacify newborns. The practice, called 'barbaric' by a nine-teenth-century commentator, survives in a modified form in the tradition of wrapping a newborn tightly in a blanket. 'Swaddled babies are experiencing the close contact they desire, without the benefit of human touch,' comments Deborah Jackson.

Mother's Little Helpers: Baby Sleeping Aids

In the 1960s my mother's East End cleaning lady gave her a tip for getting children to sleep. 'We would stick their heads in the gas oven for a few seconds, or give them whisky.' Back in the nineteenth century, children had to face even scarier treatments, usually involving opiates, as quoted in Christina Hardyment's *Perfect Parents*: 'I sell in retail alone five gallons of "quietness" and a half gallon of "Godfrey's",' a druggist in Manchester told Thomas Bull.

Mrs Beeton counsels Victorian mothers not to trust wet nurses (who usually slept in the baby's room):

The next point is, to watch carefully, lest, to insure a night's sleep for her-self, she does not dose the infant with Godfrey's cordial, syrup of poppies, or some narcotic potion, to insure tranquillity to the one and give the opportunity of sleep to the other. The fact that scores of nurses keep secret bottles of these deadly syrups, for the purpose of stilling their charges, is notorious; and that many use them to a fearful extent, is sufficiently patent to all.

Even in the enlightened twentieth century, and now in the twenty-first, the use of drugs is not completely unheard of, as Deborah Jackson points out in *Three in a Bed*. She quotes Jane Vosper, *Good Housekeeping*'s 'matron' in the 1970s:

I often wish I could prescribe a night nurse under the National Health Service, someone to take charge in the early hours while this awkward phase lasts. Some parents take it in turns for night duty … But if a weary mother always has to cope on her own, a suitable sedative can be given to the baby for her sake, say for a week at a time.

And it is not unknown for parents to abuse Calpol, for example, although giving Paracetamol to a baby nightly or in large doses can cause liver and kidney damage. Deborah Jackson quotes a *Guardian* article, in 1998, that claimed one-third of infants under the age of two were deliberately fed alcohol by their parents – sometimes to see how they reacted, sometimes to get them off to sleep.

However, most modern 'little helpers' are of a different variety. CDs of lullabies, the two-way child alarm, night lights, and teddy bears and blankets (aka Transitional Comfort Objects – TCOs) are all innocent childhood trappings – or are they? Some modern theorists, starting with John Bowlby and his cloth and wire-mesh monkey 'mothers', have seen a more sinister significance in them. Modern society, they claim, is using consumerist trappings to appease babies deprived of what they really want – 24-hour contact with mum. Let's look at a few quotes, starting with Jean Liedloff's Evil Mom in the Nursery from Hell:

> *She sighs, and puts him gently in his crib which is decorated with yellow ducklings and matches his whole room … There is a toy woolly lamb stood at a beguiling angle on top [of the chest of drawers], and a vase of flowers – which have been cut off from their roots, for his mother also 'loves' flowers … She bends to kiss the infant's silky cheek and moves towards the door as the first agonized shriek shakes his body. Softly, she closes the door. She has declared war upon him. Her will must prevail over his. Through the door she hears what sounds like someone being tortured. Her continuum recognises it as such …*

There is something deeply disturbing in this description of the child's mother – it's hard to put your finger on it till you get to the flowers. What Liedloff is implying is that this mother (who is going along with the perceived wisdom of the day, let's not forget) 'loves' her baby in the way that she 'loves' flowers – by killing them. She also accuses the mother of being a torturer. Isn't this a bit over the top?

It's worth noting that Liedloff by all accounts did not get on with her mother. She lived with her grandmother during her teens and says of her death, which eventually drove her to the jungle: 'My thoughts were not very clear during my grief at the loss of my grandmother, but because turning to my mother always ended in my being hurt, I felt I had to make a giant effort to get on my own feet.' So that's where the sadistic Western mother comes from … Liedloff also characterises her mother as having a 'brilliant and original intellect' – another good reason, perhaps, to worship the Yequana mothers who had not been perverted (in Liedloff's opinion) by

Western education. There is something patronising in Liedloff's descriptions of Yequana mothers that brings to mind Rousseau's 'noble savage'.

This is Liedloff on toys and teddies:

'The things that are put within his reach are meant to approximate what he is missing. Tradition dictates that toys be consoling to a grief-stricken infant. But it does so somehow without acknowledging the grief. First and foremost, there is the teddy bear or similar soft doll "to sleep with". The eventual fierce attachment to them which is sometimes formed is viewed as a charming bit of juvenile whimsy, rather than a manifestation of acute deprivation in a child reduced to clinging to an inanimate object in its hunger for a companion …'

> ## *It worked for me*
>
> We used to put Max to sleep in his cot with a little snuggly toy attached to a blanket. Now he loves it, and he won't go to sleep without it. I often find he's still clutching it in the morning. ***Chloe, mother of Max (1 year)***

Deborah Jackson, who might be viewed as a modern successor to Liedloff (she quotes her extensively, and has met her), has a more balanced approach to TCOs:

> *In our consumer-based society, there are many tempting ways of dealing with our children's needs for tactile stimulation and nocturnal security. Manufacturers mass-produce the cot and they even supply accoutrements to take the place of the mother, who can hardly crawl between the bars to soothe her infant.*
>
> *Many products are designed specifically as night comforters. Baby sheepskin rugs, warm and cosy, can help the baby to settle. Baby-bouncers simulate the wonderful feeling of being jogged around in mother's arms. Baby alarms monitor the infant's breathing while parents are at the other end of the house.*
>
> *But these products can't really do the trick. No teddy bear or cot-jiggler yet invented can simulate all the benefits of a mother's body. According to Dr McKenna, 'mother's biorhythms physiologically regulate their offspring both prenatally and postnatally'. Babies need their mothers, not machines.*

Whether or not toys and gadgets are mummy-substitutes, it's astonishing how attached children can get to them. If your baby or child has an attachment to a particular toy, and you know where it came from, BUY ANOTHER ONE. My nephew Felix lost his beloved Fluffy, which happened to be a Budweiser mascot from the 1980s bought in California, and if it hadn't been for the miracle that is eBay he would have been inconsolable.

~
Bath Time for Baby

An important part of the night-time ritual for modern parents is bath time –
a nice warm bath is meant to help babies settle down for the night. Yet until
quite recently it was believed that cold baths were better for them, as Christina
Hardyment describes in *Perfect Parents*:

> *Dipping in the waters of the Styx was not the inevitable fate of eighteenth
> century babies, although several manuals saw cold baths as a desirable goal
> to be achieved. For the first few weeks the bath was
> to be tepid. By slow degrees the water could get
> colder, until the child was enjoying its freezing dip.
> The baby was to be watched for signs of languor,
> and the baths discontinued in that case. 'Lively
> singing' was to accompany the experience, so
> the idea of pleasure would become associated
> with bathing.*

This continued into the early nineteenth century, when improved plumbing
made it easier to provide warm baths – although there were some parents
like William Cobbett, the early nineteenth-century journalist and author of
Advice to Young Men, who continued to believe in cold ones:

> *A great deal in providing for the health and strength of children depends
> on their being duly and daily washed, in cold water from head to foot.
> Their cries testify to what degree they dislike this.*

Even in the Edwardian era, Truby King was a fan of cold baths, but only
for children aged two and older. Babies were allowed a warm bath at 100°
Fahrenheit. The timing was not important, he felt:

The best time for bathing baby is usually just before the 10am feeding, although some mothers prefer to bath the baby in the evening. Provided one hour has elapsed since the last feeding, the time chosen for bathing baby is unimportant, but it should be the same time every day.

My mother, who was a Truby King baby, has a cold bath every morning, and says it makes her feel more healthy and alert. Perhaps a result of early conditioning?

No Sex Please, we're Parents

There is an epidemic of 'no sex' in modern families, if the media is to be believed. An article in the *Guardian* quoted Esther Perel, the author of *Mating in Captivity*, who believes couples should take a ten-day holiday from their children every year and flirt with other people to keep their marriages alive (see opposite).

The intrepid interviewer tried out some of Esther's sex tips and is able to report an increased level of bedroom activity. But children and sex have been seen as incompatible for some time – this poem was written in the sixteenth century:

> *But you, perhaps, by other cares beguiled,*
> *Wish, to the nurse's home to move the child;*
> *Because by his continued cries at home*
> *Your sleeps are broken and your joys o'ercome*

The modern attachment-parenting fans who co-sleep with their children have to deal with a lot of questions about how they manage to have sex at all – but are unlikely to respond, as Jean Liedloff does, with the comment that it might be good for babies to witness what Freud referred to as 'the primal scene':

'One can gauge the heat of an issue by the level of discomfort it generates at a dinner party. Asking if there is sex after marriage is about as bad as asking if there is life after death. I broached the question of conjugal passion after reading Mating in Captivity, the unnerving book written by the Belgian New Yorker Esther Perel ...
I may as well have thrown a grenade on the table: "Sex!" an older gentleman almost vomited the word. "I mean sexy sex is the stuff of affairs, NOT marriage."
His wife, bejewelled, beautifully dressed, intelligent, sat opposite him, unblinking. "Frilly black knickers!" he bellowed, "They're just not going to cut it after you've been ringside for the C-section."

There is concern, too, about the infant being present when his parents make love. Among the Yequana, his presence is taken as a matter of course, and I daresay it has been so, as well, during the hundreds of millennia before us. It may even be that in not being present he is missing an important psychobiological link to his parents which leaves him, or her, with a sense of longing for it which turns later into a repressed, guilt-laden Oedipus, or Electra, wish to make love to the parent of the opposite sex, when in fact he only wanted the infant's passive role in the first place ...

For most woman, though, it isn't the baby that puts them off having sex; it's switching from mummy to mistress. In France this is considered quite an issue. New mothers are given three weeks to slob around in dressing gowns covered with baby sick, then they are expected to go to the hairdresser, get into those suspenders and show their poor neglected husbands a good time.

It worked for me

Jasmine went right off sex after the birth of her baby Madeleine. 'I was breast-feeding for three months and I felt really sore and completely unsexy. My partner was very understanding and didn't pressure me, but I knew he felt left out. The crunch came when I was watching an old movie called *The Big Easy* with Dennis Quaid and Ellen Barkin, which has a very hot seduction scene. It suddenly made me remember what I was missing. I left Maddy with my mum for the night, booked a hotel room and we haven't looked back since!'
Jasmine, mother of Madeleine (4 years)

Song for a Young Mother

There, there, you fit my lap
Like an acorn to its cup,
Your weight upon my arm
Is like a golden plum,
Like an apple in the hand
Or a stone on the ground.

As a bird in the fallow
Scoops a shallow hollow
Where the earth's upward pressing
Answers egg and nestling
– Earth's mass and beginning
Of all their learning –

So you learn from my arm
You have substance and a house
So I learn from your birth
That I am not vague and wild
But solid as my child
And as constant as the earth.

E.J. SCOVELL,
FROM *POEMS AND READINGS FOR
BIRTHS AND CHRISTENINGS*

-5-

Bottoms And Burps

One thing nothing in life prepares you
for is changing your first nappy.
Unless you practised on Tiny Tears and Co.,
or did a lot of babysitting, the chances
are you'll do this for the first time on
your own first baby.

'Never wash the first nappy a baby dirties.'

'1952 HEALTH VISITOR:
"One of my mothers refused to hang her
baby's nappies out in the moonlight for fear
of bad luck."'

THE OXFORD DICTIONARY OF SUPERSTITIONS

It's a humbling process, as you realise that something that appears so, so simple can be so complicated. How can it take so long to remove one tiny set of clothes and replace them with another tiny set of clothes? You seem to have too few hands, as you try to prevent your baby trampling in its dirty nappy, or pooing on your lap, or rolling off the changing table. Then there is the problem of trying to perform this complex operation, complete with floppy-headed, precious, germ-vulnerable newborn, in hostile territory, such as a café with no available horizontal surface. After three years or so of this, having changed several thousand nappies, you will be a pro and could probably do it with your eyes closed – but then your offspring will be ready for 'toilet training', as it is optimistically called.

It was not always thus. Back in the bad old days of the early eighteenth century, babies were kept in their swaddling clothes and rarely changed at all. A Dr Cadogan is quoted in Christina Hardyment's *Perfect Parents*:

> *There is an odd Notion enough entertained about change. Some imagine that clean Linnen and fresh cloths draw and rob them [babies] of their nourishing Juices.*

But even Cadogan insisted on only a once-a-day change of nappies.

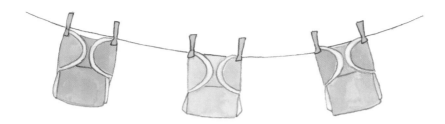

By the end of the eighteenth century, swaddling had gone out of fashion, as had the use of 'stays' under older children's clothes, and babies' poos and pees had to be dealt with, as it were, head-on. Thus began years of worry and agonising over 'motions' and how to deal with them, problems that have not been dealt with even today in the age of the nappy mountains.

Eighteenth-century plumbing, or rather the lack of it, probably had a lot to do with the period's laid-back approach to bodily excretions. Only the rich could afford to bath (in a tin or copper bath with water heated in a kettle), and chamber pots were simply emptied into the street with the cry of 'Gardy-loo!' (an anglicisation of 'Gardez-l'eau' or 'Mind the water', which evolved into 'loo'). The contents were carried away in channels that often ran down the centre of a street – in London they all went into the Thames. In cities, water was available only from public pumps.

It was the mid-nineteenth century before the 'loo', in its modern form as one piece of ceramic, appeared, although the first flushing toilet was invented in 1778. And sewerage improved dramatically when a Public Health Act that made it compulsory to have some kind of sanitary arrangement in every household was passed in 1848. Underground sewers were built, and public sanitation improved – the 'public convenience' or toilet was invented in 1858. It was at this point that handbooks that dealt with cleaning and changing babies, not to mention how often they 'went', began to appear.

Eighteenth-century insouciance about bodily functions (and sex) had been replaced by Victorian prudery, and babies, like everyone else, had to conform. In her *Book of Household Management* Mrs Beeton avoids dealing with the subject and is prepared only to give guidance on how to dress a baby:

Dress and Dressing, Washing, &c.
As respects the dress and dressing of a new-born infant, or of a child in arms, during any stage of its nursing, there are few women who will require us to give them guidance or directions for their instruction; and though a few hints on the subject may not be out of place here, yet most women intuitively 'take to a baby', and, with a small amount of experience, are able to perform all the little offices necessary to its comfort and cleanliness with ease and completeness. We shall, therefore, on this delicate subject hold our peace; and only, from afar, hint 'at what we would', leaving our suggestions to be approved or rejected, according as they chime with the judgement and the apprehension of our motherly readers.

Chavasse is a great deal more forthright in *Advice to a Mother*:

How soon may an infant dispense with diapers?
A babe of three months and upwards, ought to be held out, at least, a dozen times during the twenty-four hours; if such a plan were adopted, diapers might at the end of three months be dispensed with – a great desideratum – and he would be inducted into clean habits – a blessing to himself, and a comfort to all around, and a great saving of dresses and of furniture. 'Teach your children to be clean. A dirty child is the mother's disgrace,' [Footnote: Hints on Household Management, by Mrs C.L. Balfour] Truer words were never written, – A DIRTY CHILD IS THE MOTHER'S DISGRACE.

Chavasse claims that babies who are held out a dozen times during 24 hours could be nappy-free by the end of three months and learn clean habits. Sound unlikely? In the United States there is a movement, if you'll pardon the phrase, to teach babies how to use the potty, called elimination communication or infant potty training, of which more later. We're apparently heading back towards the type of regimen our grandparents might have adopted for their offspring.

In the nineteenth century, babies were simply held over a chamber pot several times a day (and at night). An attentive nurse or mother was supposed to be able to spot when a baby was ready to do a poo (and presumably a pee) and put it on a potty. The idea was that over time it would associate the bowel movement with the chamber pot. This is Dr Conquest, in *Letters to a Mother*:

> *An infant may be brought at a very early age to be so cleanly as to go without any guard, if regularly put on a chair, or if a little pan be placed under it as it lays on the lap. In many well-managed nurseries this practice begins so early that the necessity for napkins is almost superseded by the time the children attain the age of four months.*

So far, the process sounds relatively benign, or at least not traumatic for the child. However, the starchy food prescribed for babies and toddlers meant that

It worked for me

We all know how hard it can be to get out of the house with small children. My favourite first-year tip is to either laminate, or slip into a ziplock, a diaper bag checklist. You make a list of everything you want to have in your diaper bag, place it in a front pocket, and refer to it before you leave the house. This tip is especially helpful for dads. It helps them avoid forgetting key items like diapers and bottles when they leave the house, babe in arms! An adjunct to this tip is to place your absolute essentials (mine are: keys, wallet, cellphone and lipstick) in a small pouch that can be transferred from purse to diaper bag. This is especially helpful for working moms and moms who love handbags.
Anna, mother of Hank (6 years) and Jonathon (2 years)

many children (at least, those who were not breastfed) had digestive problems and constipation – judging by the quantities of laxatives and purgatives they were given. This meant that an element of coercion crept into the toilet training as babies were 'encouraged' to go at certain times. This is the advice of Luther Emmett Holt, author of *Care and Feeding of Children*:

> *At first there may be some local irritation, like that produced by tickling the anus, or introducing just inside the rectum a small cone of oiled paper, or a piece of soap, as a suggestion of the purpose for which the infant is placed on the chamber.*

Holt (Dr Spock's mother's guru), whose experience of babies was mostly confined to hospitals, was an extreme baby-trainer, but it is easy to see how babies coerced into performing on the potty could have developed the problems that Freud was to focus on not long afterwards.

To simplify Freud (a lot), strict toilet training during what he referred to as the 'anal phase', which doesn't allow children to be in control of where and when they poo and pee, leads to 'anal retentive' personality types who become obsessively tidy, organised, mean with money, etc. What might be called the modern approach, from Spock onwards, where children aren't given routines or 'trained' in a coercive way –'I think that the best method of toilet training is to leave bowel-training almost entirely up to your baby,' Spock said – leads to the 'anal expulsive' type: messy, disorganised and rebellious, but also creative and confident (and perhaps with a deep, suppressed yearning for order, which is why they buy all those Gina Ford books? Just a thought.).

It's not surprising, given the murky nature of Freud's insights into infant psychology, that many parents fled with relief to Spock's relaxed laissez-faire approach. I wonder what the elimination communication movement makes of the Freudian mindset about toilet training. Its gurus are usually at pains to differentiate their way of leading a nappy-free lifestyle from the rigorous routine that Freud identified as traumatic. Laurie Boucke, author of *Infant*

Potty Training and mother of three sons, is one of them. This is what she had to say in the *New York Daily News*:

> *Infant potty training is the gentle, dual practice of communicating with your baby and being responsive to his or her elimination needs. It is also called 'elimination communication'. The three main beneficiaries are babies, parents and the environment.*
>
> *When we take our little ones to a toilet place (potty or other receptacle) around the time they need to 'go,' we afford them the opportunity to practice using their 'toilet muscles' and encourage them to continue communicating. This allows them to develop elimination control –*
>
> *both muscular and neural – at the earliest moment possible. Infants are pottied while being held lovingly in their parent's arms. This is a cozy time for both parent and child.*
>
> *Since infant pottying gradually reduces diaper use, it conserves natural resources such as trees and water (with far less soiled clothing, bedding and towels, and less rinsing of baby bottoms, legs, etc.).*
>
> *It also reduces wastewater pollution, sludge, ground-water contamination, use of electricity and fuel, air pollution and bulk going into landfills.*
> (16 OCTOBER 2005)

A lot of the toilet-training controversy arises simply because no one seems certain about when babies and small children should be able to control their bladder and bowel movements. A study by T.B. Brazelton in the 1960s suggested the appropriate age to begin training them was 18 months ('later is better'), and this has remained the standard for some time. According to one of my baby books, other ways of finding out when a toddler was 'ready' included watching to see whether it could climb stairs using alternate feet.

A Belgian study of toilet training over the last 60 years (published in 2000) shows how things have changed in terms of when, and how quickly, a child is trained. Three groups of parents of different ages were interviewed, and the study found that the type of 'bladder training' that was carried out in the 1940s (encouraging a child to stay dry during its afternoon nap, for example) helped to prevent 'lower urinary tract dysfunction' (involuntary peeing) later.

However, a 2004 study in America, published in *Pediatrics*, suggested there isn't much point to all this angst and early training:

Conclusions. Early initiation of intensive toilet training correlates with an earlier age at completion of toilet training but also a longer duration of toilet training. Although earlier toilet training is not associated with constipation, stool withholding, or stool toileting refusal, initiation of intensive training before 27 months does not correlate with earlier completion of toilet training, suggesting little benefit in beginning intensive training before 27 months of age in most children.

This is useful ammunition if you have the kind of mother-in-law who talks rather pointedly about how all her children were potty trained before they could talk.

When I mentioned elimination communication to my mother, she told me about her childhood in China and how small children wore trousers with open crotches to facilitate early training. These are now being sold as training aids on websites like www.mummysmilk.com, which also stocks a T-shirt saying, 'The best way to diaper is to Un-diaper'. It is interesting that many cultures such as those of China and India achieve earlier training than we do, and apparently with a lot less anguish. Here's Jean Liedloff on the Yequana baby (diaper-free, obviously), in *The Continuum Concept*:

'When house training does take place at the age of about two, the toddler is chased outside if he sullies the hut floor. By that time he is so thoroughly accustomed to feeling and being considered right, or "good", that his social impulses, as they develop, are harmonious with those of his tribesmen.'

Before house training the Yequana mother's response when her baby pees or poos on her is apparently is to 'laugh heartily' and hold it away from her body. Still, as Liedloff points out, 'water sinks into the dirt floor in moments and excrement is cleared away immediately with leaves'. Not an option for the twenty-first-century mum, then, unless you are really eco-friendly and living in a yurt … Liedloff contrasts the Yequana baby to the modern American baby at his or her nappy change (usually 'his', in Liedloff's world):

'As the infant matures and his cognitive
faculties awaken, he becomes aware of a
difference in his mother's manner when she
discovers his diaper needs changing.
She makes a sound of a clearly rejecting sort.
She turns her head to the side in a way
which shows she does not like cleaning
and making him comfortable.
Her hands move brusquely and with
the very least possible contact.
Her eyes are cold, nor does she smile.
As awareness of this attitude sharpens,
the infant's pleasure at diaper-changing time,
at being attended, touched and having his
chronic, mild case of diaper rash
temporarily relieved, becomes mixed
with a bewilderment which is the precursor
of fear and guilt.'

~
The Nappy

The ancient Egyptians, Aztecs and Romans used milkweed-leaf wraps, animal skins and other materials for nappies. Eskimos put moss under sealskin clothes, and some native American tribes put grass under rabbit skin. The English word 'diaper' is the ancestor of the United States diaper – it originally meant 'linen' and was first referred to in Shakespeare's *The Taming of the Shrew*: 'Another bear the ewer, the third a diaper.' In Elizabethan times the linen was wrapped around the baby in 'swaddling bands' and probably changed only every few days. Swaddling was swapped for 'diapers' in the eighteenth and early nineteenth centuries. 'Nappies' comes from baby 'napkins'.

Nappies were held on by loops, or were sometimes sewn on, or fastened with a flannel 'pilcher' over the top. Dr Conquest, a mid-nineteenth-century doctor, said of the pilcher that it tended to 'heat and enfeeble the loins, as well as inducing diseases of the lower spinal marrow and rendering the child prone to paralysis'.

The invention of the safety pin by Walter Hunt, in the United States in 1849, was a giant step in the history of nappy design. Mrs Beeton criticises the 'abominable use' of pins in children's clothing, but as her *Book of Household Management* was published only ten years later, in 1859, she was probably still referring to ordinary pins. Hunt also invented the sewing machine, but his seamstress daughter told him it would put women out of work and he abandoned it. He sold the patent for the safety pin for $400.

Industrial weaving processes made cloth nappies cheaper and more readily available. They were first mass-produced by Maria Allen in America in 1887, and by the end of the nineteenth century babies in both the United States and Britain were wearing squares of fabric fastened with safety pins.

Nappies had to be changed frequently (the cloth gets waterlogged very quickly, as would-be eco parents know) and, of course, they had to be washed by hand. In *Domestic Duties* (1825) Mrs Parkes recommends six dozen in a layette. The number had halved by the early twentieth century – Truby King recommended three dozen. Like Dr Conquest 60-odd years before him, in his *Feeding and Care of Baby* he worried about the effect of nappies on a child's development:

> *The napkin, though used as a protection to the clothing, is itself one of the most important of the baby's garments. If applied too 'snugly', or tightly, or if allowed to extend down nearly to the knee, or if made too bulky and bunchy, the napkin hampers free exercise, and is liable to give rise to grave deformities of the pelvis and legs. To avoid these objectionable features, when the square napkin is folded into a triangle, only one thickness should be pinned up between the legs, the other being folded back under the buttocks.*
>
> *... The use of waterproof pilchers should be condemned. Baby's napkin should be changed directly it becomes wet or soiled, but if these pilchers are worn the napkin may be wet for some time before it is discovered. The waterproof pilchers thus act as a poultice, and are apt to cause irritation of the buttocks.*

It worked for me

I had my two children ten years apart. My first child was out of nappies by the time she was two years and three months. It was all quite painless. But my second child stayed in nappies till she was three and a bit. I was worried that she would be the only child at primary school still wearing Pampers! I wondered whether the difference was due to their very different personalities, but actually I think the reason is more straightforward. In the ten years since I had my first child disposable nappies have become so much better that there is simply no incentive for children to get out of them. If you really want to potty train a child early, put it in terry nappies. **Debbie, mother of two**

Macintosh fabric, named after its inventor, was patented in 1823. Judging by the number of babycare writers who criticised using it with nappies, it must have been popular! The problem was leakage and the need to constantly change the baby. During the 1930s 'Cell-Stoff', a soft cellulose tissue, was created in Germany as a substitute for imported cotton. A Swedish company, Pauliström Bruk, built on this to make a soft parcel that could be placed in a baby's knickers. By 1941 this had become a two-piece product called a 'disposable diaper': the pad of cellulose wadding was covered with knitted mesh or gauze, was disposable and came with a reusable outer pair of knickers.

However, the norm in the early to mid-twentieth century was cloth nappies fastened by safety pins, just as it had been in the nineteenth century. Americans started to use diaper-washing services during the Second World War, when mothers worked in factories. Washing machines became popular in the United States in the late 1950s and early 1960s. They were slower to catch on in Europe (although the first one was patented in Britain in 1691), and women continued to wash nappies by hand, just like my mother did.

The Mothercraft Manual of 1948 gives instructions on how to wash nappies. It recommends Harrington Squares ('As used in the Royal nurseries', the advertisements claimed). Folding them was also an art mothers learnt early on. It's hard to see how they found time to do anything else, after reading this:

To wash. Put to soak in cold water, keeping wet and soiled ones separate. Wash the wet ones in plain water. Treat the soiled ones as follows: Brush off all faecal matter, soak in cold water, rinse in warm water, scrub with Primrose soap to remove the stain, rinse in fresh warm water, rub on fresh soap, boil for ten to fifteen minutes and rinse in three waters. Napkins should be boiled daily, preferably in the morning so they can be hung out in the open air. If quite impossible to boil, wring out and pour a kettle of boiling water over them. Never use soda, strong soaps, blue or any bleacher. A pair of little woollen drawers or a pilch should be worn outside when the baby is being carried. These are less bulky and easier to wash than the old-fashioned flannel pilches.

By this time disposable nappies were on the horizon in the United Kingdom – although Dr John Gibbens gives them only a brief mention in his *The Care of Young Babies*:

A few words now on napkins. They can be put on in two ways, in the traditional English triangular way with one safety pin holding everything together in front; or in the continental fashion with a pin at each hip. Probably you will find the triangular way is better during the early months, the pin at each hip method better later on when the baby is a little older. Two napkins are usually wanted at first, the soft muslin one next to the baby, the Turkish towelling one over it as an extra precaution. Over these two layers of napkins many mothers nowadays use waterproof knickers which pin up at either hip … there is nothing against them if they are for occasional use only, and if they fit loosely enough for plenty of air to circulate round the baby. In some countries, Sweden for example, a baby wears a thick pad of cellulose padding next to the skin and over that a pair of plastic pants … It is simple and practical, and a perfect boon when on holiday … You can also buy disposable napkinettes, but they are fairly expensive, although a few packets are very handy when you go on a holiday or visit a friend.

Finally, Gibbens goes on to recommend 'napkin services':

In London and some other large cities it is now possible to join a napkin service. For a few shillings a week they take away all the dirty napkins and bring them back to your door next day spotlessly clean and beautifully laundered.

What a relief that must have been to mothers who were used to scrubbing nappies, rinsing them three times and boiling them every day …

~~~~~~

Movies with Memorable Nappy-changing Scenes
Baby Boom
Three Men and a Baby
Jack and Sarah
Ghostbusters 2
Look Who's Talking

~~~~~~

In the United States, the development of the disposable nappy became an American entrepreneurial success story. In 1946 Marion Donovan, an enterprising housewife and mother of two who came from a family of inventors, was dissatisfied with cloth nappies and invented the Boater, a waterproof covering that she improvised from a shower curtain and fastened with snaps. This was used with a conventional cloth nappy. A year later, she modified her design and added disposable absorbent material. Although she could not find anyone to take it on (manufacturers thought it would be too expensive to produce) she went into business for herself and eventually sold her company for $1 million.

Meanwhile a year later, in the United Kingdom, Scotswoman Valerie Hunter-Gordon, eventually a mother of six, invented a disposable nappy which was manufactured as the Paddi Pad. Her third child, Nigel, born in 1947, starred in the advertisements. Once the era of the disposable had begun,

It worked for me

Nappies: disposable is the only way. We have tried everything else and they all suck. Moltex Oko or Nature aren't so bad [for the environment] in any case.
Andrew, father of Amelie (5 years) and Hazel (2 years)

parents weren't going to look back. The design was refined as the bulky original was slimmed down following improvements in sanitary-towel technology, and the first gesture at an eco-friendly disposable nappy was invented in the 1980s. The basic design was in place, and steadily became cheaper and more popular.

However, disposable nappies have their own costs, even while they free mothers from back-breaking nappy duty. These are some sobering statistics on the United Kingdom's nappy habit from the Women's Environmental Network:

Cost
Home laundered nappies could save parents around £500 on the cost of keeping a baby in nappies.
You can kit out your baby in real nappies on the high street for under £50. This includes all the nappies and waterproof covers you need for the whole of your baby's nappy wearing life. The same amount of money would only buy 7 weeks of disposables …
Waste
Nearly 3 billion nappies are thrown away in the UK every year. The vast majority of these (90%) end up in landfill.

There are also health worries. Will the chemicals used in (most) disposable nappies affect a baby's health? Do baby boys suffer impaired fertility if their genitals are overheated? We don't know whether these questions will seem as bizarre to future generations as the worry that too much study makes adolescent girls infertile, or that bulky nappies lead to rickets, which might

It worked for me

If you want to go eco, but don't want the hassle, don't be afraid to combine cloth and paper. Use cloth at home, but carry disposables when you go out. I did this with my first, and both my conscience and my diaper bag stayed clean.
Anna, mother of Hank (6 years) and Jonathon (2 years)

have kept our grandmothers awake at night (if they took the experts seriously). It's possible that our worries are nonsense, and it is also possible that in a decade or two they will be established as babycare gospel. If this book tells you anything, it should be that even scientific information can be as biased, misleading, culturally determined or just plain 'wrong' as any old wives' tale.

~

The Bottom Inspectors

The women talked with passionate interest about stool color and formulas, colic and its causes: they compared notes, offered helpful hints and admired each other's children. It was as if there existed a secret sisterhood, an underground movement to which anyone could belong who had a baby. Any new women who strolled past with infants in carriages were easily welcomed, were immediately friends. But there was almost never any conversation about anything else.

This definitely defines a parent. You were never interested in things scatological before (unless you were an alt.perv Internet type). But when you have a baby you discover a new, absorbing topic of conversation as the extract above, from Marilyn French's *The Women's Room* shows. Who knows that newborns have orange poo, for example? No one until they have their first baby. As Chavasse sternly warns, a baby's nappies are a pretty useful indicator of its state of health:

THE BLADDER AND THE BOWELS OF AN INFANT.
Have you any hints to offer respecting the bowels and the bladder of an infant during the first three months of his existence?
    A mother ought daily to satisfy herself as to the state of the bladder and the bowels of her child. She herself should inspect the motions, and see that they are of a proper colour (bright-yellow, inclining to orange), and consistence (that of thick gruel), that they are neither slimy, nor curdled, nor

green; if they should be either the one or the other, it is a proof that she herself has, in all probability, been imprudent in her diet, and that it will be necessary for the future that she be more careful both in what she eats and in what she drinks. She ought, moreover, to satisfy herself that the urine does not smell strongly, that it does not stain the diapers, and that he makes a sufficient quantity. A frequent cause of a child crying is, he is wet, and uncomfortable, and wants drying and changing, and the only way he has of informing his mother of the fact is by crying lustily, and thus telling her in most expressive language of her thoughtlessness and carelessness.

In *The Nanny Diaries* Nan, the heroine of this best-selling exposé of life as a nanny to the rich and famous, describes being interviewed by a woman living in New York's Upper East Side who keeps a written record of her baby's nappies and their contents next to the cot. Nan sees this as obsessive, but if you are demented by lack of sleep and simply cannot remember how many times your newborn has wet its nappy, a written record may seem to be the only way to go. Otherwise, how will you know whether your baby is eating and drinking enough? You're already trying to remember how much he/she fed, how long for and when it was. But at least you aren't being terrified out of your wits by Truby King:

Abnormal Motions

*1. **Green motions**. Greennness is commonly a sign that the bowel-contents are being hurried on too quickly ... [it] should put the mother on her guard to avoid any possible source of digestive upset, such as over-feeding, irregular or too frequent feeding, tainted milk, too strong or wrongly portioned milk mixture ...*

*2. **Curd in the Motions**. Mothers are apt to worry themselves unduly about the presence of a little curd in the stools. Usually it is of little consequence ...*

*3. **White, tough, pasty bulk motions** are apt to occur where babies are fed on unmodified or merely diluted cow's milk ...*

4. **Pale, clay-like motions** *may be due to deficiency of bile, arising from obstructed bile duct or disordered liver.*

5. **Hard, dry, or crumbly motions** *indicate constipation.*

6. **Brown, black or red motions.** *Bleeding into stomach or bowels causes brownness, blackness or redness, according to the site of the haemorrhage. Black motions are normal in the first week of life, and may also be caused by drugs. Brownish motions are a normal result of starch or starchy patent foods.*

7. **Thin watery motions** *are common in diarrhoea, but are most marked in rare choleric summer diarrhoea, tending to rapid collapse.*

8. **Frothiness and foulness of motions** *are evidence of abnormal fermentation which may call for washing-out or irrigation of the bowel.*

9. **Slime or mucus in the motions.** *A certain amount of mucus is present in all normal stools. Much slime and mucus … may be the herald of acute dysenteric diarrhoea, leading to blood and pus in the motions followed by rapid poisoning of the system, torpor and collapse. Much jelly-like mucus, associated with the presence of worms, may be present as a chronic condition in weakly dyspeptic children.*

Talk about too much information … ! Although some of the scarier and more dangerous purgatives, of which more later, might have left the nursery

It happened to me

When my younger daughter was six months old she became very constipated. The textbooks and the local nurse told me not to worry – constipation was very common in babies. But Alice was also beginning to cry a lot, which was unusual in such a placid baby, so I took her to the hospital. They dismissed my worries but I insisted they take a closer look. Good thing I did, as it turned out Alice had a bowel obstruction that needed immediate surgery. If I had waited even another 24 hours her chances would have been slim. Always trust your instincts about your baby. *Amy, mother of Catherine (16 years) and Alice (14 years)* by the early twentieth century, scrutiny of nappies continued. In *Perfect Parents* Christina Hardyment quotes a description of a doctor 'visiting' his baby patients at the Boston Floating Hospital in 1954:

> *The professor carried a wooden spatula in his breast pocket which was used to smear the specimen of stool, to note its consistency, to search for curds – soap and beans; with never a look at the infant, but only from this meticulous examination, on which he would expatiate lengthily and eruditely, he would finally offer suggestions for the next day's food.*

This kind of professor doesn't seem very far from Augusten Burroughs' demented adoptive father, Finch, in *Running with Scissors*, who believed his bowel movements were messages from God:

> *When Finch received a windfall in the amount of one thousand dollars from the insurance company, he took this as a definite sign that the turd had, in fact, been a direct piece of communication from the Heavenly Father. As a result, he scrutinized each of his bowel movements …*

The fact is, changing nappies and monitoring their contents is something that becomes second nature when you've been doing it for a while, but is unimaginable beforehand. The average parent changes over 2000 nappies per child …

This is what Louise Wener of the pop band Sleeper had to say in the *Guardian* about becoming a mum:

'My own mother gave up having a career to raise three children. As a child I thought her a slave to domesticity. I feared turning into one of those women, the kind that leap up from behind the coffee urn at mother and toddlers mornings – coated in baby sick and parsnip puree — to harangue you for not using eco-friendly nappies. I craved freedom, independence, adventure, excess; a world away from the domestic landscape of marriage, mortgage and kids. I've long since settled down to monogamy and property repayments but having a child seemed like the final frontier. I would be a pram pusher, a bottom wiper, manacled to the kitchen sink, a hostage to bottle feeds and bath times. But all that was a failure of imagination on my part. Domestic life is merely the backdrop to becoming a parent.'

(25 April 2006)

~
Staying Regular:
Toilet Training by the Book

When a baby is first born it usually has meconium, a dark green substance, in its system. This caused a lot of anxiety in the nineteenth century and was usually purged by some kind of (unnecessary) laxative. This was only the start of a lifelong regimen for some unfortunate babies. The number of 'aperient' medicines, etc. that were considered necessary up to and including the twentieth century is amazing.

The worst culprit was grey powder, or calomel, which was used for stomach disorders. It was actually a poisonous mercury compound that could gradually kill a child. As late as the 1940s, John Gibbens was advising against using it as a 'teething powder': 'There is evidence that mercurial purgatives given repeatedly – the teething powder given every Friday night – may do harm.'

Purgatives or laxatives were generally overused and Chavasse, like many other doctors in the nineteenth century, argued against them, saying that just a little castor oil or magnesia should be given when absolutely necessary:

> *Before concluding the first part of my subject – the Management of Infancy – let me again urge upon you the importance – the paramount importance – if you wish your babe to be strong and hearty – of giving him as little opening physic as possible. The best physic for him is Nature's physic – fresh air, and exercise, and simplicity of living. A mother who is herself always drugging her child, can only do good to two persons – the doctor and the druggist!*

He does, however, give a recipe for a castor-oil dose that includes dill water (an addictive soporific – maybe that was why it was so popular as a nursery remedy):

The dose will depend upon the age and the known effects of aperient medicine upon the child, some requiring more, others less. As a general rule, one or two tea-spoonfuls. To cover its unpleasant flavour it may be given in various ways: either mixed in warm milk, or floating on peppermint, mint, or some other aromatic water. Or, if the stomach is unusually delicate, it may be made into the following emulsion, of which give a dessert-spoonful or more, according to the age, every hour until it operates: Take of castor-oil, six drachms; the yolk of an egg; dill-water, two ounces; loaf-sugar, two drachms; mix intimately.

Even in Truby King's time there was an emphasis on being 'regular':

It is of the utmost importance to insure regularity of the bowels. Try to get them to move at the same time every day just after the morning and afternoon feedings. In a very young baby the disturbance may cause some food to be put up, but usually this tendency soon ceases. If training be begun early, regularity can usually be brought about by the second month.

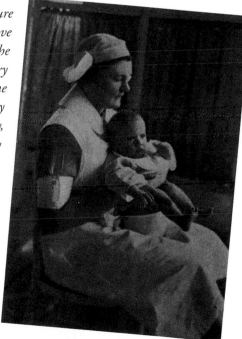

If a baby's 'training' was unsuccessful and it didn't respond to being put on the potty in the morning, King suggested the use of a 'soft rubber catheter, size XII' or the 'soft rubber nozzle of a small "bulb" enema', specially made for babies', containing salt water.
I shudder to think of the struggles between mothers and babies as a result of this advice.

By John Gibbens's time – the 1940s – things had loosened up a bit, so to speak:

At first a baby has no control whatever over bladder or bowel – the train of events is fired off as soon as the tension within reaches an uncomfortably high level. But he is quick to learn the pleasures of feeling dry and warm, the discomforts of lying long in wet sodden napkins: and if you change him quickly whenever his napkin is wet or dirty, it will only be a matter of weeks before he lets you know he needs changing by his cries. This is the secret of training – to make a habit pleasurable ... Since the bowels act less frequently and the baby gives some warning that he is about to have an action by straining and going red in the face, it is easier to train him to the use of the pot. Some babies with highly developed nervous systems have such frequent motions that early training is impossible ... but others may pass 1–2 motions daily as regularly as clockwork, and then you should certainly get the baby to associate in his mind the passing of a motion with the feel of the pot.

John Gibbens's instructions are a lot more palatable to a modern reader than those of earlier experts, and I was amused to read his descriptions of a baby punting around the room on its potty. (His solution was to give it a book or toy and tie it to a table leg with a scarf for ten minutes 'to get on with the job'.) By eight or nine months, Gibbens claimed, a baby could be left with nappies off for two hours in the morning, and by ten months for two hours in the afternoon as well. By the age of a year to 18 months 'many babies, if they are potted several times a day, can dispense with napkins during their waking hours'.

It's certainly true that modern parents do perhaps ignore this issue and mindlessly use nappies for too long. My sister Tabitha didn't realise her younger son was staying dry all night until she accidentally put him to bed without a nappy. According to *Contemporary Pediatrics* magazine, 50 per cent of the world's children are potty trained by the age of one. But the research is contradictory and whether Western parents should consider taking on early potty training is a bit of a poser. As many of the 'diaper-free' organisations admit, elimination communication demands a lot of extra attention from a carer and is probably incompatible with the needs of most working parents. Here is what Tina Kelley has to say in 'Fast Track to Toilet Training for Those at the Crawling Stage' (*New York Times*):

'Unquestionably, in a child-rearing culture that thrives on sanitation and parental convenience, the prospect of supervising 20 deposits a day in the first busy months of infancy is daunting. "It doesn't sound like anything I would ever attempt to try," said Erinn Marchetti, who has two preschool-age children and was shopping recently at Toys "R" Us in Times Square. "It's hard enough when they're 2 and 3."'

(9 OCTOBER 2005)

However, fans of the elimination communication method claim it is more hygienic, enjoyable for the baby and parent, and helps bonding.

An Ill Wind

Wind took me by surprise. I had vaguely realised there was a point to all that patting and rubbing, but was stunned by how much I was supposed to do and how often the baby needed it. I'd start 'winding' her, and literally forget what I was meant to be doing and stop before the job was done. I very soon realised that carrying her in a sling removed the problem, or at least minimised it, and took to 'baby-wearing' as one way of avoiding the boring process. This is Philippa de la Haye on the subject, in *Green Parent*:

It's good for your baby's health
Newborn or premature babies who are carried in a sling against their mother's body adapt to the environment outside the womb more quickly. The close contact helps to regulate their body temperature, heartbeat and respiration.

Being held in an upright or semi-upright position can help some babies with wind or colic. If you carry your baby in a sling for a while after feeding it can help them to get any wind up and prevent any pain caused by it passing through their system.

Wind wasn't mentioned much in early books and only started being dealt with in the Victorian era, when prams and separate cots meant a baby was no longer held in its mother's or nurse's arms for long periods and was spending more time flat on its back.

Truby King has some advice about winding, but it carries a sting in its tail! Notice the emphasis on not playing with or handling baby unduly: he was meant to spend time with 'his natural playmates, his hands and feet' rather than with adults.

Handling Baby After Feeding
After he is fed, and perhaps during the course of feeding, baby should be held upright against the shoulder and gently patted on the back to enable him to expel wind swallowed during suckling.

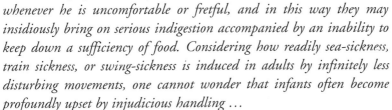

After making sure that baby is warm and dry you should place him in his cot to sleep, and on no account should he be played with or handled unduly, as this may cause vomiting.

Generally, the less handling of the baby, the better. 'Habitual patting on the back, done at any time of day, is highly injurious,' King states:

Many women thoughtlessly and almost mechanically pat a baby to soothe him whenever he is uncomfortable or fretful, and in this way they may insidiously bring on serious indigestion accompanied by an inability to keep down a sufficiency of food. Considering how readily sea-sickness, train sickness, or swing-sickness is induced in adults by infinitely less disturbing movements, one cannot wonder that infants often become profoundly upset by injudicious handling …

Babies have been sent to our Baby Hospital suffering from emaciation, vomiting and grave nervous debility, due almost solely to this one factor. The same mother has been known to encounter similar difficulty in rearing child after child, and has arrived at the conclusion that her progeny had some grave inborn tendency to vomit, until the contrary was proved by removing the latest arrival to the charge of a quiet, sensible, trained baby nurse.

Phew! What a relief all round … One wonders what Liedloff's Yequana baby, who is used to spending its time being joggled around by its mother while she dances or runs through a sudden shower of rain, and who is then doused in a river, would make of the Truby King baby's lifestyle.

John Gibbens has some rather more balanced advice:

'Wind, one of the bugbears of infant feeding during the first few months of life, is nothing more than swallowed air. It is normal for every baby to swallow down air mixed with his feeds, whether he is breast-fed or bottle-fed, but if you sit him up immediately after his feed and rub his back gently, he will bring up the air in two or three gulps, and then he is ready to be laid down in his cot. Unless you help him to bring up his wind, the swallowed air will pass through the stomach to the intestines, causing abdominal distension, colicky pains and screaming. Helping the baby to bring up wind needs gentle handling, time and patience, otherwise he is apt to bring up milk as well as air. Some babies need as much as 15–20 minutes to bring up their wind.'

Modern advice has nothing very different to add, except for the tip about keeping babies in a sling to modify wind.

Top tip for new grandmothers: never tell a mother who is cooing over her baby's first smile that it is 'only wind'. It goes down very badly indeed.

The Little Boy and the Old Man

Said the little boy, 'Sometimes I drop my spoon.'
Said the old man, 'I do that, too.'
The little boy whispered, 'I wet my pants.'
'I do that too,' laughed the little old man.
Said the little boy, 'I often cry.'
The old man nodded, 'So do I.'
'But worst of all,' said the boy, 'it seems
Grown-ups don't pay attention to me.'
And he felt the warmth of a wrinkled old hand.
'I know what you mean,' said the little old man.

SHEL SILVERSTEIN,
ESSENTIAL POEMS FOR CHILDREN
BY DAISY GOODWIN

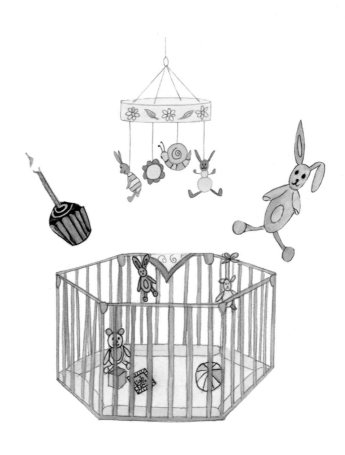

-6-

Raising The Perfect Child

*Once the first cavewoman mother had fed her
baby son, wrapped him in an animal skin
and put him to sleep, she probably sat down
with her partner and said, 'What now?
Do you think he'll grow up to be a hunter?
Will he be better with a bow and arrow, or a
spear? Or maybe just sit around the cave all
day grunting like you …'*

'As the twig is bent, so the tree's inclined'
ALEXANDER POPE

Once the basics of survival – food, shelter and warmth – have been attained, and assuming that a child is healthy, new concerns about development, moral and spiritual welfare and intellectual capabilities start to creep in.

Parents who until relatively recently were grimly resigned to as many as half or more of their children dying young could not help but be very aware of their children's spiritual needs, while modern parents, obsessed with education, competition and material well-being, sometimes seem uninterested in moral values or instilling self-discipline. But the general trend has always been first to ensure a baby's physical survival and good health, and only then to worry about its intellectual development and welfare – concerns that were more those of the rich, or reasonably well-to-do, than of the poor.

Bath Time: 'Dip them into the waters of the Styx'

Even activities like bathing, which would seem purely practical, had inbuilt 'values'. For example, William Cobbett, the early nineteenth-century journalist and writer, made his offspring take cold baths to improve their health; singing was to accompany these to help them associate bathing with pleasure (I suspect babies were too smart to be fooled by this – perhaps they were put off singing as a result). The French philosopher Jean Jacques Rousseau suggested children should be dipped 'into the waters of the Styx' to harden them: in other words, the more harsh experiences they faced, the tougher they would be. In Sir Frederick Truby King's day babies were spared cold baths (although their warm ones were still rather Spartan, with no toys or 'dawdling' post-bath) –

but they were to be introduced to a 'cool sponge after the bath' as training for later on, as he describes in *Feeding and Care of Baby*:

> *This is stimulating and invigorating, and teaches the child to take a cold shower later on in life. Begin with water a few degrees cooler than the bath, and gradually lower the temperature, until the water used for sponging is 60 deg. F – say at the end of the year. If baby becomes blue or cold discontinue the cool sponging for a time.*

I love the matter-of-fact 'If baby becomes blue'. This regimen must have been a nightmare in countries that were colder than New Zealand, and one can only hope that mothers didn't take it too seriously. By the time Mabel Liddiard's *The Mothercraft Manual* was published in 1923, a 'few minutes play' was allowed for baby; toddlers in their cold baths were probably only too keen to get out. It is a relief to turn to Dr John Gibbens's advice in *The Care of Young Babies*, first published in 1940 (he is one of the very few early twentieth-century writers to assume that fathers might want to be involved):

> *The bath is given comfortably warm, at about 100 degrees. At first most mothers use a baby bath, though quite soon a baby is ready for the grown-ups' bath, which has several advantages It is much quicker, you don't have to carry water about, and the baby can splash about freely to his heart's content. In England it is customary to soap the baby on your lap … but abroad they do things differently. They spread a towel on a bed, or place a mattress and towel on a low-lying table, and there they soap the baby before dipping him into his bath, and there they dry and dress him after his bath. This method gives you greater freedom to use your hands, it makes it easier for a father to bath and change your baby – and all fathers should learn to become expert at both – and there is no chance of a slippery baby wriggling off your lap like an eel. Babies love baths and they will splash about and laugh and enjoy themselves*

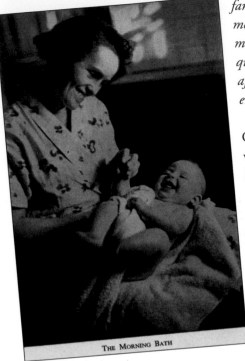

THE MORNING BATH

famously; it is quite one of the best moments of the day. In summertime many babies 4–5 months old like a quick sponge over with cold water after their bath; others will even enjoy a cold bath.

Gibbens makes the obvious point that when it is really hot children may well like having a cold bath, but in any other kind of weather this is obviously unsuitable. And it's nice to see babies being allowed to enjoy their baths. By the time Dr Spock was writing his *Baby and Childcare*, the emphasis was on making bath time fun, rather than seizing the opportunity to stiffen moral fibre:

It worked for me

Before I had my first baby I went to a parenting class at my local hospital and was shown how to give a baby a bath using a doll. I duly bought a baby bath. But bathing a doll and a screaming wriggling baby are two different things. I was terrified that I would drop Scarlett. In the end I just got into my big bath and got my husband to hand me Scarlett. She was quite happy lying on my chest while I splashed her with water. We went on having baths together till I had my second baby. The only thing I would say about having a bath with your baby is that in the first few weeks you need someone to hand you the baby and to take the baby from you when you get out. Slippery baths and small babies can be a lethal combination. *Natalie, mother of three*

Most babies, after a few weeks' experience, have a wonderful time in the bath. So don't rush it. Enjoy it with him.

In *The Continuum Concept*, Jean Liedloff describes how Yequana mothers dipped their babies into rivers:

> *The Yequana take advantage of the baby's predisposition to this sort of performance and, keeping his rules and respecting his go-ahead signals, dip him into more and more challenging waters. A daily bath is routine from birth, but every infant is also dipped into fast rivers; first only his feet, then his legs, then his entire body. The water goes from swift to swifter and onto plunging rapids and falls, the time of exposure lengthens too, as the baby's response reveals growing confidence.*

Dipping a baby into a swiftly moving river was an education game that helped it learn about water (the Yequana are excellent canoeists) while the daily bath (also in the river) was a more leisurely and sensual affair:

> *Once a day each woman put her gourds and clothing ... on the bank and bathed herself and her baby. However many women and children participated, the bath had a Roman quality of luxuriousness. Every move bespoke sensual enjoyment, and the babies were handled like objects so marvellous that their owners felt constrained to put a mock-modest face on their pleasure and their pride.*

Here again, the emphasis is on the baby's physical enjoyment of the bath and although the river game sounds frightening, Liedloff states that the Yequana respected the baby's own 'rules', unlike the scary childcare theorists of the nineteenth and early twentieth centuries. The mothers bathed with their children and enjoyed touching them. Nowadays, many baby books recommend having a stress-free bath with a newborn, but I imagine this would not have occurred to Dr Spock, who was very much a creature of his time.

The Art of Dressing Baby

Clothing a baby was another way of teaching it values while also answering a practical need. For example, as this extract from Hugh Smith's *Letters to Married Women* shows, patience was a virtue for the nineteenth-century baby:

> *Even at this tender age, the little creature may be taught to be patient, and even gay, under suffering. Let it be remembered that every act of the nurse towards the infant is productive of good or ill upon its character as well as its health. Even the act of washing or clothing may be made to discipline and improve the temper, or to try and impait it, and therefore may be very influential on its happiness in future life.*

In 1835, in *A Treatise on the Diseases of Children*, Dr Michael Underwood inveighed against fashionable clothes for infants, and invoked 'nature' as a guide to how children should be dressed. At this point swaddling had been abandoned, along with 'stays' (corsets) for female children, but babies still had to wear 'binders' around their stomachs as well as various other items of restrictive clothing.

Nature knows no other use of clothing but to defend from the cold; all that is necessary, therefore, for this purpose, is to wrap the child up in a soft loose covering, and not too great a weight of it; to which ornaments enough might be added without doing mischief. And had this matter been always left to the most ordinary discretion of parents, this is probably all that would have been done; but the business of dressing an infant has become a secret, which none but adepts must pretend to understand. The child itself, however, discovers to us the propriety of such clothing, by the happiness and delight it expressed every time its day-dress is removed, and its night-clothes put on, which are looser, and less thick than those worn throughout the day, and the lower limbs less confined. The art of dressing has laid the foundation of many a bad shape, and, what is worse, of very bad health through the greater part of life. Instead, therefore, of a scrupulous and hurtful attention to such formalities, nurses would be much better employed in carefully examining new born infants, in order to discover any malformation of those parts, especially concerned in the excretions necessary to life, which have sometimes been strangely overlooked.

Dr Underwood was very pro-child, exclaiming against cold baths (and particularly complete immersion in cold water, which was apparently done by some parents) as barbaric. It's easy to see that the values which are being invoked here are those of health and nature, as opposed to fashionable discomfort and misery. This was part of a move towards 'rational clothing' which began in the nineteenth century (partly spearheaded by Amelia Bloomer, the inventor of trousers for ladies) and led to the formation of the Rational Dress Society in 1881. It decreed that women should wear only 7 pounds weight of underwear, rather than the 14 pounds that had been the average in the 1850s (who weighed the underwear to find out, I unfortunately cannot tell you).

As in the case of the Empire style of dressing (which was more relaxed than the trends that preceded and followed it), fashions that influenced women filtered down to children.

Truby King also put the emphasis on health and nature:

> *In planning baby's wardrobe the first need is for practical comfortable garments which give the maximum of wear and use as the baby grows. The following essential points in regard to baby's clothing must be kept in mind.*
>
> *To ensure light, warm, porous, non-irritating materials.*
>
> *To get warmth and air without undue weight or multiplicity of garments.*
>
> *To see that the garments are made in such a way as to ensure easy washing, drying and ironing.*
>
> *To have no constricting bands (to hinder development).*
>
> *To have no undue double thicknesses of material (difficult to air well).*

Truby King's babies were to be well-ventilated and able to move freely (so that they could develop physically). Hygiene was important, and in fact was almost a moral virtue with King (who was himself notoriously slovenly and untidy). Practicality and cheapness were also a theme, which made sense, I imagine, for his target audience of busy housewives but also seems to reflect an anti-luxury, anti-fashion feeling on his part. It's almost as though too much focus on a baby's beauty or attractiveness was part of the 'coddling' King so heartily disapproved of and wanted to prevent.

He disliked fashion for fashion's sake, and *Feeding and Care of Baby* includes photographs of feet deformed by unsuitable shoes. One shows the feet of three women, describing them like this:

> *A) Feet markedly misshapen, but deformity much below average. These comparatively undamaged feet belong to an imbecile, who has not had the opportunity of indulging her vanity!*
>
> *B) Average civilised woman's feet [not a pretty sight]*
>
> *C) Excessive, but not rare, distortion [worse]*
>
> *We cannot too strongly appeal to parents to do all in their power to protect*

the rising generation from the physical VICE of deformed feet. Let us start with the babies.

I can't help feeling that these descriptions reveal Truby King's general feeling that women are worse than 'imbeciles' … Another fault he rails against is changing from one style of garment to another, for example:

> … *changing from homely flannel to embroidered cotton finery for exhibition purposes, taking a baby out of a warm, stuffy cot indoors and wheeling him about in a push-cart with bare arms and uncovered, dangling legs.*

Pushcarts – an early type of buggy that allowed a baby to sit up rather than a hooded pram in which it could only lie down – were a pet hate of King's because babies couldn't sleep comfortably in them. His book shows a tot slumped over in his pushcart, in a head-on-chest position parents will probably recognise.

By Dr Spock's time a baby's basic wardrobe had not altered that much, except that Spock suggests subscribing to a diaper service 'if you can afford it'. He recommends no buttons and tapes on shirts (presumably press studs, which were first used on gloves in the nineteenth century, had made it into babywear?) and warns against overheating babies in warm rooms. 'Too big' is better than too small, he says, and big openings for the head are better, so as not to make a baby 'frantic' when dressing and undressing him (for early Spock as, interestingly, for Liedloff, baby is always 'him' unless they are specifically referring to little girls). Babies don't like caps, he says (accurately!), and bootees and stockings are unnecessary until a child is up and playing; and 'dresses make a baby look pretty, but are unnecessary otherwise, and bothersome to the baby and the mother'.

It's hard to know what Spock and King would make of today's baby clothes, which come in such vast numbers and colours. The strangely puritanical tone of the anti-fashion brigade continues in today's eco-parenting guides, which extol the virtues of natural dyed organic cotton, second-hand clothes and hemp. It's absolutely true that a baby doesn't 'need' expensive garments, and I am a huge fan of second-hand ones, but surely there should be room for a little parental pride in a child's appearance? I'm not advocating a Posh-like obsession with clothing it head to foot in designer togs, but I look forward to the day when all eco-friendly options are as attractive in terms of fashion (and, if possible, price) as high-street baby clothes.

There is another way, of course, as the first issue of *Mother and Baby* magazine, in 1956, reminds us:

'With nine happy months to plan for baby's trousseau mother-to-be can, if she is skilful with sewing and knitting needles, make most of the garments baby will need. A resourceful mother does not need to resort to expensive shops to gather together all the pretties she wants for her baby's trousseau.'

In these days of disposable baby clothes the idea of creating something unique for your baby is rather attractive. Luckily, knitting patterns today are a lot easier to follow than those printed in *Mother and Baby* for a Simple Layette (which include one for 'Pilch Drawers', whatever they may be!).

~ Sunbathing: 'All young creatures need the sun'

Sunbathing is an aspect of early twentieth-century babycare that is particularly interesting in terms of changing mores. Edwardians and their descendants felt as strongly about the sunbath as their Victorian forebears did about the cold bath. This is what Truby King has to say on the subject:

> *Keep the baby in the open air as much as possible. A sun-bath does not stop at the surface – radiant energy penetrates the body and stimulates the vital processes.*

At this time sunshine was seen as health-giving, rather than the skin-ageing and cancer-stimulating baddie that it was later exposed to be. This was because of its ability to stimulate the body's production of Vitamin D and so help to cure rickets, which was caused by a lack of this vitamin. Rickets was a huge problem at the beginning of the twentieth century. Called the 'slum swellers' disease, it was the inevitable result of cramped housing conditions and poor nutrition. Even today, people are diagnosed with Vitamin D deficiency due to lack of exposure to sunshine. However, it gives one pause to reflect that Truby King was recommending that a baby's skin be exposed to sunshine in increasing doses in order to tan it – essentially the opposite of the advice we have today. The obsession with fresh air and sunshine must have led to some sunburnt babies, although King does suggest that the best times for sunbathing are earlier and later in the day. Special outfits were to be worn, to expose as much of a baby's skin as possible to the sun's health-giving rays.

Even in the 1959 edition of Gibbens's *The Care of Young Babies*, sunbathing is still being championed:

> *All young creatures need the sun, for it is their natural element. A skin tanned brown by sun and air is proof against most of the ills that flesh is heir to, yet while many mothers are willing enough to let their babies have a course of artificial ultra-violet light at a hospital [clearly a common treatment in those days], many are reluctant for babies to be out in the natural ultra-violet light of the sun.*

Gibbens suggests that sunbathing should begin at one to two months, with five minutes on the front and five minutes on the back, rather like a piece of toast. It's certainly a contrast to the modern advice, which is to cultivate the pallor of Nicole Kidman and offspring in *The Others* at all times … I've seen babies out for a stroll in sun hats and sunglasses, and with sunshades. To quote Patsy in *Absolutely Fabulous*: 'God, I miss the ozone layer.'

~
Bouncing Babies

It may seem odd to talk about babies and exercise in the same breath (don't they move around enough once they learn to crawl?), but the subject has been a concern for a long time. Eighteenth-century parents discouraged crawling, feeling it emphasised the 'animal' nature of childhood, and many used little go-carts, sometimes with wheels (they looked rather like modern baby-walkers). By the nineteenth century children were allowed to crawl around and were carried in front of open windows to have 'air baths'. Baby exercisers that appeared around this time included the Roger's Infant Gymnasium, a precursor to the modern baby-bouncer.

Most importantly, the pram had been invented by the 1850s and was popularised by Queen Victoria. Of course, a baby could not exercise its own body in one, but it could 'take the air'. In *Perfect Parents* Christina Hardyment argues that the invention of the pram was in a way a distancing device, like

the invention of the nursery and the role of the nursemaid. It allowed parents to spend time away from their small children and also allowed them to be cared for without constant contact. Jean Liedloff has a similar argument against prams, which she disapproves of for the same reason that she disapproves of playpens, harnesses and cribs – they 'imprison' babies:

'At these times he can see the white plastic corner inside a baby carriage and sometimes, when he is turned face-up, the sky, the inside of the carriage hood and occasionally great blocks which stand at a distance and slide past him. There are distant tree tops, nothing to do with him either, and sometimes people looking down at him and talking, to one another usually, but sometimes to him.'

Her advice (it's worth noting at this stage that Jean Liedloff never had children of her own) is to carry the baby and put the shopping in the pram:

The problem of shopping is mostly one of having a capacious shopping bag and not buying more than one can carry at once [hence, lots of trips, but a continuum concept mother isn't working]. It would not be a bad idea, as long as there are so many baby carriages in the world, to put the shopping in them and carry the baby. There are also back carriers for babies which have straps over both the adult's shoulders and leave her hands free. They are on sale in many department stores.

Spock, too, disapproves of prams for older children, but allows harnesses:

> *Keeping an able-bodied walking baby tucked in his carriage may keep*
> *him out of trouble, but it cramps his style and hinders his development.*
> *Some parents find a harness is very practical for shopping and walks at*
> *this age. It should not be used for hitching him in one place for long.*

There aren't many reins today (although they did sell out briefly after the Jamie Bulger case). Now that they are outlawed, modern parents tend to use prams for a lot longer than Spock ones did, if we're to believe the 1957 edition of *Baby and Child Care*. There are more cars to contend with, not to mention low-lying supermarket shelves stuffed with chocolates.

The big debate is between facing-backward and facing-forward pushchairs. Should your baby look at you or the outside world? Supporters of the facing-forward version say it gives it a chance to interact with the outside world and develop its independence; the facing-backward camp feels it should be able to see its mother at all times. I feel that, if forced to choose between these two alternatives, Truby King would have wanted his babies to face the outside world whereas Jean Liedloff would have had them gazing at their mother.

Liedloff talks in a mystical way about newborns 'discharging their energy' through physical contact. Yequana babies have more 'muscle tone' despite their apparent passivity and softness because of the way they are constantly held in arms.

Truby King would have had none of this nonsense. His babies are encouraged to exercise in a manly and vigorous way:

> *A large amount of exercise should be taken, from a very early age, in the*
> *form of vigorous sucking, kicking, waving the arms, etc. and later on by*
> *crawling. Every such activity should be encouraged. At least twice a day*
> *the infant should have for fifteen or twenty minutes the free, unhampered*
> *use of his limbs. In warm summer weather, if protected from wind by a*

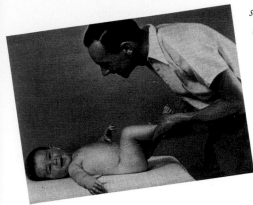

screen, a fairly strong baby may be laid on a bed or rug in the open air on a sunny verandah, clad merely in a woollen shirt, long stockings and napkin. Here he may be left to kick freely and enjoy himself for five or ten minutes… As baby gets older, he learns to take more and more exercise; first, rolling and tumbling about, then crawling, and finally standing and walking.

'Sturdy and Strong': Truby King's Hidden Agenda

There is a point to the Truby King regimen, as he states clearly in the Formation of Character section in *Feeding and Care of Baby*:

The mother should never forget that the destiny of her baby (bodily and mental) is mainly determined in the first years of life … If the mother fritters away this one golden opportunity instead of making the most of it and doing the best possible for her baby, no after care can make up for her mistakes or neglect … The fostering of sound, regular, hygienic organic habits and self-reliance at the earliest possible age not only establishes such habits for life, and promotes the growth of the parts immediately concerned, as well as the health of the body generally, but will also manifest its influence on higher planes. Tendencies trained early into the very tissue and structure of the simpler and more primitive vital organs will assert themselves later on in assisting the development and functioning of the most complex and peculiarly human parts of the organism upon which character, control and conduct to a large extent depend.

Why was it so important for children to grow up regular, hygienic and self-reliant? 'Hardy' is a word that was used a lot. With his schedules and rules, Truby King places a strong emphasis on obedience, as though a baby were a well-trained soldier. Some commentators have remarked on his 'imperialist' cast of mind, but it's worth digging a little deeper to see what is meant by this.

In 1925 King sat on the board of a committee in New Zealand that examined the problem of 'Mental Defectives and Sexual Offenders'. The group explained the 'Origin and Scope of its Enquiry':

> *For a considerable time there has been a growing feeling of anxiety among the public owing to the number of mental defectives becoming a charge upon the State, and also the alarming increase in their numbers through the uncontrolled fecundity of this class. Furthermore, owing to the frequency of sexual offences, many of a most revolting character, there was a strong demand that some action should be taken to prevent further acts of this nature; it being suggested that the law should be altered to make it possible for surgical operations to be performed upon these offenders.*

The problem was that the 'feeble-minded' were outbreeding the brighter members of society:

> **Section 1.–A Menace to Modern Civilization.**
> *The Committee are of the opinion that the unrestricted multiplication of feeble-minded members of the community is a most serious menace to the future welfare and happiness of the Dominion, and it is of the utmost importance that some means of meeting the peril should be adopted without delay. The position is the more serious because, while the feeble-minded are extraordinarily prolific, there is a growing tendency among the more intellectual classes for the birth-rate to become restricted.*

In other words, Truby King's babycare agenda fitted into a wider framework that can be called 'eugenic theory': improve the race by weeding out potential bad apples. Both the theory and practice were widespread during the early twentieth century. Techniques for improving the race included controlling the birth rate among less desirable members of the population (contraception or even sterilisation), encouraging a higher birth rate and lowering the infant mortality rate among the more desirable members, preventing physical deformities or sicknesses which were seen as tending to weaken the racial stock, and curtailing 'moral depravity' (which was seen as a sign of being

'feeble-minded'). For example, according to King, masturbation in babies and children was a 'serious vice' that needed 'medical attention' as quickly as possible. His promotion of birth control among the working classes, role as the director of a mental hospital, livestock breeding and child-rearing theories can be seen as being of a piece with his interest in eugenics. As someone who was blind in one eye and had had tuberculosis, and whose wife suffered from rickets and was unable to bear children, Truby King was not a believer in the extreme forms of eugenics, but he was interested in improving the race.

Sir Francis Galton, the founder of eugenic theory, was a distant cousin of Darwin and was influenced by him. The idea was that different races, and different types within each race, compete for success, and that it is better for the weak not to reproduce. Some eugenicists (inaccurately) understood Darwin's theory of evolution to mean that a physical problem that developed in one generation might be handed down to the next (they thought acquired characteristics could be hereditary, hence the concern that bodies should be kept healthy). Eugenics promotes aggression and competition (hence the emphasis on hardiness) but Truby King also wanted 'mental' and 'moral' values to prevail (hence the emphasis on obedience and regularity). These are the conclusions of the society, which he put his name to:

New Zealand is a young country already exhibiting some of the weaknesses of much older nations, but it is now at the stage where, if its people are wise, they may escape the worst evils of the Old World. It has rightly been decided that this should be not only a 'white man's country', but as completely British as possible. We ought to make every effort to keep the stock sturdy and strong, as well as racially pure.

Truby King's theories became popular in Britain after conscription was introduced during the First World War. The authorities were shocked to find that conscripts from poor urban areas were in such poor physical condition that they were unsuitable even to be cannon fodder. The average British soldier was a full 15 centimetres (6 inches) shorter than his Canadian counterpart. (The height of an individual is genetically determined, but national heights reflect a country's health. The Dutch, who have one of the best antenatal systems in the world, are the tallest nation in Europe.)

The government of the day realised that steps had to be taken if British babies were eventually to become model soldiers. Hence the popularity of Truby King and his emphasis on hardy individualism. Baby clinics were set up in poor areas and a network of health visitors was established. It was the first time the government had become involved in bringing up baby, but not by any means the last: the Sure Start programme introduced by Tony Blair's Labour government is all about raising model citizens.

~

Baby Breaks Free

Like Truby King, but much cheerier, John Gibbens was also a nursery philosopher, emphasising the importance of 'training' to prepare a child for the 'lesson of life':

The great lesson of life is self-control and discipline; and is not nursery routine simply preparation for life? Training is a means by which you pass on to your child your deepest convictions, the quintessence of all you believe in, the lessons that you yourself have learned from life. Only by training can you spare the child the dangers into which he must inevitably drift …

To care for babies and young children successfully comes easily to some mothers, but not to all. It needs:-

A genuine love of children, with understanding of the greatness and high adventure of the world into which they are born.

Patience and faith in the future.

Firmness of purpose to stick stoutly to what you believe to be right.

A quick eye to note when a baby is ready to make a fresh stride forwards.

A sense of humour.

If only one could be such a paragon … At least Gibbens had high, rather than low, expectations of mothers. He also understood that babies need to exercise their minds as well as their bodies:

'Babies like the companionship of grown ups. They don't like to be left alone too much, they need comforting and cuddling, they like to be spoken to and sung to. So enjoy your baby, take him about with you when he's awake, sit him up in the corner of an armchair and let him watch you going about your household duties.'

In other words, a baby is not a little machine. He or she is a person with needs, such as avoiding the boredom of staring at a white ceiling for hours. Like Liedloff, Gibbens was a great admirer of non-Western peoples (back to nature, yet again):

In some parts of the world you will come across races, such as the Sikhs and the Pathans, where every man carries himself like a god — upright, fearless, with flashing eyes and superb bearing; and this superb posture has been achieved by exercise and an open air life. From the very first, then, your baby needs freedom to use his arms and legs, freedom from the restraints of swaddling clothes, freedom from the excessive use of cot and pram which crimp and curb all activity.

PUT ON THE FLOOR TO EXERCISE AT SIX MONTHS OF AGE.

At last, baby was to be freed from solitary confinement!

Milestones: Rolling, Crawling and Walking

In *The Care of Young Babies* Gibbens identifies the milestones of baby development, such as rolling and crawling, and gives instructions on how to play with a baby (note play, rather than 'exercise') during each phase. Truby King also recognised milestones, which are helpfully set out in diagram form in *The Mothercraft Manual* by his disciple Mabel Liddiard. Milestones were first identified in the late nineteenth and early twentieth centuries when babies were first observed scientifically. There is nothing particularly unusual or objectionable about them, but it is worth noting that they appeared without the disclaimers used in modern manuals (such as 'every baby is an individual'). So women had a new worry, about developmental stages and whether their children were ahead or behind in the race to toddlerhood. 'Keep up!' You can almost hear the baby gurus urging children (and their mothers) on.

It worked for me

After I had my first baby I bought a book called *What To Expect The First Year*. At the beginning of each chapter there is a section about what your baby should be able to do at the beginning of each month. But it doesn't just stop at a simple list of accomplishments like controlling the head and sitting up, it suggests things that a presumably A-stream baby may be able to do – 'recognisable sounds' at seven months and 'advanced small motor skills' at eight months. Every time my perfectly normal bright baby failed to reach one of these advanced baby milestones I would feel quite dejected. I began to feel we were both failures, even though by normal standards my baby was doing brilliantly. Luckily for my peace of mind I dropped the book in the bath and all the pages stuck together. Without that insane checklist I was much happier. I really think some baby books should come with a health warning. *Sasha, mother of two*

'Let Him Out When He's Had Enough': the Playpen

Once a baby passed the crawling 'milestone', it was time to find a way to keep it safe while its mother got on with her chores …

Finally comes the great day when he finds he can creep forwards, and now you'll have to be careful, for he will be in the coal box in a flash and all your books will be tumbled out of the nearest bookshelf. Nothing is sacred. His energy is demoniacal, he pokes and pries into everything to satisfy his curiosity. At this stage you will need a playpen, for it is not safe to leave him alone. He may bellow at first at this restriction of liberty, but he'll soon discover the fascinating pastime of pulling himself up by the bars and later of walking round the pen holding on. When he can

'It is a good idea to procure a playing pen:
one with a floor a few inches off the
ground is best or a canvas base can be
made, which is cheaper. Cover with a
blanket or washable rug, and leave the
child in this to follow natural instincts.
At about six months of age the child
usually begins to sit holding the bars, to
roll over, and so on. At this age he should
be out on the floor outside the pen and
encouraged to kick and roll over. Get into
the habit of leaving him alone in the
room when safely in the pen; it is so
much better for
children not to be
always amused. In
summertime the pen
can be put on a rug
in the garden.'

TRUBY KING

do this, he's ready for his first steps in walking. You lift him up and take him by the hands and walk backwards while he staggers towards you. Soon he's walking unaided, and another milestone in life has been passed.

Any parent with a crawling baby knows the 'demoniacal' energy described by Gibbens, and it is certainly true that the playpen is a boon when you are running to answer the phone or the doorbell. However, Truby King's use of it for solitary confinement might be questionable (see previous page):

This reminds me of a splendid quote from a Victorian matron (not Queen Victoria herself, but it could easily have been) in Christina Hardyment's *Perfect Parents*:

Infants up to the age of one year should be neither amusing nor amused.

It's extraordinary how much has changed over the last century!

Spock approves of the (limited) use of playpens:

Let him out of the playpen when he insists. One child is willing to stay in the playpen, at least for short periods, as late as a year and a half.

Let him out when he's had enough.

Another thinks it's a prison by the time he's 9 months. Most like it well enough until they learn to walk, around the age of a year and a quarter. I'd say let your baby out of the pen when he feels unhappy there. I don't mean at the first whimper, for if you give him something new to play with, he may be happy there for another hour …

As far as Liedloff is concerned, the playpen is a tool of the devil. She gives a long account of a Yequana father who 'invented' one:

It was nearly finished when I noticed Tududu working on it. It had upright sticks lashed with vines to an upper and a lower square frame, like a comic strip version of a prehistoric playpen. It had cost a good deal of labour and Tududu looked quite pleased with himself when he lopped off the last protuberant stick-end. He cast about for Cananasinyuwana, his son, who had taken his first step about a week earlier. No sooner had Tududu sighted the tot than he snatched him up and put him triumphantly in the new invention. Cananasinyuwana stood uncomprehendingly for a few seconds at the centre, then made a move to one side, turned about and realised he was trapped. In an instant he was screaming a message of utter horror, a sound rarely heard from children of his society. It was unequivocal. The playpen was wrong, unsuitable for human babies.

Tududu pulls the baby out, lets him run away to his mother and then smashes the playpen to bits with an axe, accepting it as an affront to the continuum. Liedloff explains that babies have a natural sense of self-preservation that we violate by trying to control their movements:

When he goes about on hands and knees, a baby can travel at a fair speed. Among the Yequana, I watched uneasily as one creeper rushed up and stopped at the edge of a pit five feet deep which had been dug for mud to make walls. In his progress about the compound, he did this several times a day. With the inattentiveness of an animal grazing at the edge of a cliff, he would tumble to a sitting position, as often as not facing away from the pit. Occupied with a stick or stone or his fingers or toes, he played and rolled about in every direction, seemingly heedless of the pit, until one realised that he landed everywhere but in the danger zone.

Liedloff also believes that trying to protect a baby, for example by saying, 'Don't go over there where I can't see you!' suggests to the child that it should do the very thing you are trying to prevent it doing (which explains some of my children's behaviour …). However, I don't think many people would agree with her comments on the tragic death of a toddler by drowning:

> *A case in point is one of a family I heard of who were nervous of the danger their swimming pool presented to their small child. The idea was not that the pool would rise up and swallow the child, but that the child might, as well as not, fall or throw himself into the pool. They had a fence built around the pool and kept its gate locked.*
>
> *Very possibly the logical mind of the child (not the part that reasons), assisted by explanations from his parents, grasped the suggestion of the fence and the locked gate. He comprehended so well what was expected of him that, finding the gate open one day he entered, fell into the pool and drowned.*
>
> *When I heard this story which was told me to show that children need constant guarding from their own ability to harm themselves, I could not help thinking of that pit in the compound at Wanania where the children played unsupervised all day without incident.*

Wee Care: Baby-proofing

Liedloff appears to suggest that attempts at baby-proofing or minimising risk are unconscious suggestions to a child that it should try and hurt itself. In fact, she says so clearly when she quotes research from the burns unit of London's Hospital for Sick Children, stating that most burns are the result of 'emotional problems' at home, such as a difficult parent–child relationship:

> *Unconsciously using the weapon of expectation to suggest to the child that he burn himself, and perhaps helping by leaving the boiling soup in an unusually reachable position as a further suggestion, the unhappy mother can preserve the necessary virtuous front and at the same time punish herself with guilt.*

Hey! It's all mom's fault! It's hard to feel any surprise at Liedloff's conclusion …

That baby-proofing invites children to hurt themselves is a pretty radical (some might say, bonkers) idea in the context of today's safety-conscious and risk-averse society. Take the following quote from www.childalert.co.uk, a company that sells safety products for the home:

> *2 children each day in the UK die in their homes and each year more than 500,000 children aged 4 and under need hospital treatment following accidents in their home …*
>
> *If your baby or toddler is …*
> * *between the ages of 0–18 months*
> * *has begun to crawl or showing the signs*
> * *is a younger brother or sister to your toddler*
> * *is attending a play group or nursery*
>   *then Childproofing is a must for you and your family.*
>   *Childproofing is regarded as 'the greatest child safety measure since the car seat'.*
>
> *By appointment, a Childalert Childproofing expert will visit your home and conduct a safety survey with you, pointing out all the potential dangers. During the survey we will give you written advice on how best to make your home more child friendly.*

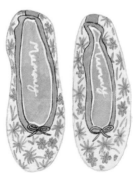

This reminds me of an episode in *The Simpsons*, 'Bye Bye Nerdie', where a child-proofing expert comes to Springfield and terrifies Marge and Homer by pointing out the dangers that face Maggie in their home:

Lady: Your baby is dead! [Homer and Marge react with horror.] That's what you'd hear if your baby fell victim to the thousands of death traps lurking in the average American home. [Shows Marge her details.]
Marge: Springfield Baby Proofing?
Homer: Y– you really scared us!
Lady: Sorry about that. But the truth is, your baby, Maggie Simpson, is dead! [Pause.] Dead tired of baby-proofers who don't provide a free estimate!

Homer initially appears to favour the Liedloff approach to child safety:

'HOMER: That baby-proofing crook wanted to sell us safety covers for the electrical outlets. But I'll just draw bunny faces on them to scare Maggie away.
MARGE: She's not afraid of bunnies.
HOMER (ominously): She will be.'

Eventually Homer himself becomes a baby-proofer, running a company called (a convincingly horrendous baby-company name) 'Wee Care'. However, when the entire baby-proofing industry in Springfield is thrown into decline, creating mass unemployment, he returns to his work in the nuclear power plant.

How to keep a child safe can become a question loaded with angst. It might be useful to go back to Rousseau in the eighteenth century to find the intellectual roots of Liedloff's 'noble savage' approach to childcare (his imaginary hero, Emile, in the book of the same name, is not 'brought up' as a conventional gentleman but is allowed to run free in natural surroundings):

Fix your eyes on Nature, follow the path traced by her. She keeps children at work, she hardens them by all sorts of difficulties, she soon teaches them the meaning of pain and grief ... One half of the children who are born die before their eighth year ... This is nature's law; why try to contradict it? ... Experience shows that children delicately nurtured are more likely to die. Accustom them therefore to the hardships they will have to face ... Dip them into the waters of the Styx.

As I mentioned earlier, Rousseau's interest in child-rearing did not extend to his own children, whom he cheerfully handed over to the tender mercies of the local orphanage.

Crying

Why do babies cry? Like Freud's 'What do women want?', this is a question that successive generations have puzzled over, no doubt while 'walking the floor' at 3 a.m. with an inconsolable, screaming baby in their arms. Dr Michael Underwood, author of *A Treatise on the Diseases of Children*, published in 1835, was a particularly acute observer of babies:

Perpetual crying, especially the perpetual recurrence of crying in infants not wont to cry much, must, on the contrary, always be taken to denote some continued, or recurrent, uneasy or painful sensation ...

Violent crying denotes, of course, violent pain. But it is frequently the mere effect of passion; the discerning physician will, however, readily perceive the difference. In some instances violent crying has led to convulsion ...

The crying is also sometimes checked, apparently by the occurrence of a sense of suffocation from the violence of the effort itself; in other cases, as in disease of the heart, the crying is checked still more promptly and suddenly. Sometimes the little infant is literally too feeble to cry …

These observations may be taken as useful hints. Still, it is the habit of carefully observing every change in the little infant, which is what I would most earnestly recommend be cultivated. Many of these changes are very important and easily detected, yet too slight to admit of description. If the child cries … be assured that it is not well.

Here Dr Underwood describes crying in mainly physical terms. What problems does it indicate? A mother should be carefully scrutinising her baby for problems. He doesn't concern himself with psychological problems. Mrs Parkes, another early nineteenth-century observer of babies, takes a similar view in her *Domestic Duties*. A baby's cry is its alarm call:

The cry of an infant should never be disregarded; it is Nature's voice.

However, also in the early nineteenth century, in *Physical Education, or the Nurture and Management of Children*, Samuel Smiles raises the possibility that babies need to cry for exercise:

Instead of being feared, the practice of crying in children in want of muscular exercise is most beneficial in its effects. Sickly and weak children cry a good deal, and but for this, it is almost certain that they could not live long. The very first act that a baby performs at birth is to cry, and many of them continue to do so at an average rate of four or five hours a day during the first years of their existence. It cannot for a moment be imagined that all their cries arise from a feeling of pain. It would be an anomaly in the benevolent working plan of creation and an unmerciful infliction of pain on the little innocents, were this the case. Not at all. They cry in default of exercise, or rather, for exercise.

Smiles suggests that a crying baby is perhaps just stretching its lungs. If so, there was less need for a parent or nurse to respond immediately – which would have been convenient in the age of the nursery.

By the early twentieth century, the behaviourists were taking a much more no-nonsense approach towards crying. It was a conditioned response, and could be trained out of a child, as with the method Dr Luther Emmett Holt describes in his *The Care and Feeding of Children*:

'How is an infant to be managed that cries from temper, habit, or to be indulged? It should simply be allowed to "cry it out". This often requires an hour, and, in some cases, two or three hours. A second struggle will seldom last more than ten or fifteen minutes, and a third will rarely be necessary.'

And this is what J.B. Watson had to say in 1928 about the crying (or non-crying) child, in his *Psychological Care of Infant and Child*:

> *The happy child? A child who never cries unless actually stuck with a pin, illustratively speaking.*

I like 'illustratively speaking'. Watson seems to be such an out-and-out scientist I wouldn't put it past him to try sticking a pin into the child to see if it cried …

Spock had a modified version of the 'cry it out' method, made more palatable for anxious parents, but the mood was changing in the 1950s as psychologists started to take a more child-centred approach. Nowadays, an uneasy mix of 'cry it out' and 'attachment theory' is available for confused parents to choose between. I quote Gina Ford (see opposite).

You can either accept Gina Ford's reassuring routines in *The New Contented Little Baby Book* and get baby Gina'd, or you can leap to comfort it at every cry, as recommended by attachment theorists like Aletha Solter in this extract below from 'Crying for Comfort: Distressed Babies Need to be Held' in *Mothering* magazine:

> *The term 'cry it out' refers to the practice of leaving babies in their cribs without picking them up, and letting them cry themselves to sleep. A modified version of this approach is to go to the baby every few minutes to pat her on the back or reassure her verbally (but not pick the baby up), and to increase the length of time gradually so that the baby eventually 'learns' to fall asleep alone.*
>
> *But there is no doubt that repeated lack of responsiveness to a baby's cries – even for only five minutes at a time – is potentially damaging to the baby's mental health. Babies who are left to cry it out alone may fail to develop a basic sense of trust or an understanding of themselves as a causal agent, possibly leading to feelings of powerlessness, low self-esteem, and chronic anxiety later in life. The cry-it-out approach undermines the very basis of secure attachment, which requires prompt responsiveness and sensitive attunement during the first year after birth.*
>
> (JANUARY/FEBRUARY 2004)

'Obviously all new parents are anxious to make their newborn baby's introduction to the world a happy one. As we all associate crying with pain or unhappiness I can understand why, as a new parent, you will be prepared to do almost anything to stop your baby crying. A newborn baby's only way of communicating is by crying, and it is important that you do not fall into the trap of thinking the only way of dealing with crying is by feeding your baby ... I would like to reassure you that provided your baby has been well fed, and that you have followed the routines regarding awake periods and wind-down time, your baby will not suffer psychological damage.'

GINA FORD

Unfortunately, the Ford and Solter approaches are more or less incompatible, so it's decision time. In the end, I think parents choose what works best for their baby and themselves …

Kissing and Cuddling

'There are rocks ahead for the over-kissed child'

J.B. WATSON

It is extraordinary that so many respected childcare theorists spent a lot of their time urging mothers not to kiss, cuddle or play with their babies. I don't think this is worthy of much more response than the one quoted in Christina Hardyment's *Perfect Parents*:

> *Would not an unkissed, rigidly hygienic baby have a very cold little soul? Would it not miss the tenderness? And how could it ever be loving and tender to anyone itself it if had never been fondled and fussed over?*
> KATHLEEN BURRELL, *THE LITTLE FOXES*, C. 1900

It would be interesting to know what psychological effects the 'no kissing' advice had on people who applied it to their babies (although surely not many did?). But one of Watson's sons committed suicide at the age of 40: who knows if this could have been due to his 'rigidly hygienic' upbringing? It must have been a great relief to parents when this particularly nonsensical theory was dispensed with, after attachment-theory thinkers like Margaret Ribble in her 1943 *Rights of Babies* and, in 1951, John Bowlby in a World Health Organization study, *Maternal Care and Mental Health*, publicised the fact that babies would literally 'pine away' and die when untouched and unloved, even if their other physical needs were provided for.

Whole Duty of Children

A child should always say what's true,
And speak when he is spoken to,
And behave mannerly at table:
At least as far as he is able.

ROBERT LOUIS STEVENSON

-7-

Girls And Boys Come Out To Play

As this book shows, childcare manuals
are as subject to the vagaries of fashion
as hemlines.

What are little girls made of?
What are little girls made of?
Sugar and Spice and all things nice,
That's what little girls are made of.

What are little boys made of?
What are little boys made of?
Slugs and Snails and puppy-dogs' tails,
That's what little boys are made of.

It's possible almost to date the moment that gender equality became a norm rather than a special interest by looking at baby manuals – in the older ones, anything up to about 1960, although the pictures are generally genderless the baby is always 'he'. Even Dr Spock adhered to this rule until the 1970s when he rewrote his classic work, *The Common Sense Guide to Baby and Child Care*, and alternated 'he' and 'she' in response to feminist criticism. The caregiver, meanwhile, is always 'she' or 'the mother', if not 'the nurse', although there are some instructions for fathers, usually given in a joking way. It seems that humour was the only way to make the child-rearing medicine go down at all as far as fathers were concerned, although everyone felt free to lecture mothers.

What Are Little Boys Made Of?

Although most of Sir Frederick Truby King's instructions in *Feeding and Care of Baby* refer to 'baby' or 'he', a few points are aimed specifically at either male or female babies. At this age, there isn't a lot of distinction between the two. Here are some of Truby King's comments on boys and girls:

Error XXII That there is a special risk in allowing a male baby to cry, as the strain tends to cause rupture.

This fallacy often makes mother and nurse nervously anxious to prevent crying. Hence they give the baby his own way day and night, and he soon becomes a spoiled, exacting, fretful little tyrant. If he cries he is given what he wants, whether it be food between mealtimes, or cuddling in his mother's bed when he ought to be asleep in his own cot. Both the digestion and the nervous system may be more or less ruined in this way.

The fallacy must have been rather nice for boy babies!

Error XXIII That in the case of female babies the nurse should massage or 'break down' the breasts so as to soften them and promote future development.

Much harm and no good results from this extraordinary proceeding. It sometimes causes abscess, and, without doing this, may so injure the parts as to prevent proper growth of the breast, and predispose to flat nipples and inability to suckle.

Babies are often born with milk in their nipples because they have emerged from a hormone bath, and it was traditional to try and extract what was seen

It worked for me

I had a son after my two daughters and I was determined that he should be brought up in exactly the same way as they were. I never bought him toy soldiers or anything that felt like a 'boy toy'. I was feeling pretty smug until I found that he had cut the hair of his sisters' Barbie dolls and had made them 'guns' out of biros and elastic bands. The result was so sinister that I caved and immediately bought him an Action Man. However much we try and influence them to the contrary boys and girls just want different things. So the politically correct parent should watch out. *Amy, mother of three* as unnatural, even 'devilish'. Notice how important it is that the baby's breasts are not damaged; they are essential to her future role as a Mother of Empire.

Finally, foreskins. I'll spare you too much detail, but Truby King did not believe in circumcision except when medically necessary. However, he did advocate retracting the foreskin, as did many early commentators, during the first month. This totally unnecessary interference would damage it, and probably led to the later problems that encouraged parents to circumcise. Again, worries about masturbation often led to circumcision, as King points out:

> *Largely on account of an impression that circumcision tends to lessen the tendency to masturbation in boys, this operation is much in vogue nowadays, and parents are greatly exercised about the question. In the writer's opinion there are not sufficient data to warrant the conclusion that circumcision should be practised as a mere matter of routine. Indeed, there are reasons for regarding the normal foreskin rather as a protection and safeguard than as necessarily a source of danger.*

Truby King's adherence to Nature's way was probably a good thing for many little boys, although there is still a lot of controversy around this issue … By Dr John Gibbens's time, the 1940s, fiddling with the foreskin at any stage of development was firmly discouraged as damaging to the child. In *The Care of Young Babies* he states firmly that there is no link between circumcision and morality in later life.

King hardly differentiates between boys and girls, apart from the purely physical comments quoted above. Because of his emphasis on robustness,

his regimen makes no concessions to the fairer sex, and all babies are to be treated and clothed alike. Even nappies are the same. It's interesting to compare this set-up to the modern one, where babies are colour-coded from birth and given 'boy' and 'girl' rooms, nappies, clothes, accessories and toys. Clearly the gender difference in little babies is a lot more important to us than it was to Truby King's generation: I wonder why? Even *The Mothercraft Manual*, which gives advice on what toys should be played with at age-appropriate stages, is silent on which ones are suitable for boys and which for girls.

King's tone is spookily similar to that of feminist thinkers of the 1970s, who believed young children were conditioned into conforming to gender stereotypes. An example is my Aunt Miranda, who taught both her boys to knit and sew! But while he wanted all babies to have an equal chance of a healthy life, he certainly wasn't advocating that men and women should be treated equally in later life.

What Are Little Girls Made Of?

Dr Leslie George Housden was heavily influenced by Truby King. He wrote *The Art of Mothercraft* specifically to teach little girls how to be future mothers:

Today you are starting a new subject – Mothercraft – differing from your other studies in a very important aspect. Your other lessons have been arranged to teach you how to play a useful part in the world at large. Reading has enabled you to take advantage of the written thoughts of men and women more gifted than yourself, to learn of the actions of other people and other nations in all parts of the world ... But mothercraft is something apart. It is of all your studies, the most personal. Through it you will learn to be happy in your own home. This is the purpose of Mothercraft teaching. It is to teach you enough about babies and small children so that when, one day, you are lucky enough to have one of your own, he will not worry you with his baby-ways, as he would if you did not understand them, and you will be able to bring him up, healthily and happily, on your own knowledge, without having to run every few days to a grannie, or a doctor, or a welfare centre, to ask them what to do next.

For Housden, as for Truby King, little girls were future mothers; they were not out there 'in all parts of the world', but were safely in their own homes. There is no mention of father.

In the late Victorian era, girls and boys dressed very differently, and behaved very differently, from an early age. In 1878, in *Advice to a Mother*, Chavasse implored parents not to allow them to dress 'like men and women' (which meant the nightmare of 'stays' or corsets for little girls):

Have you any general remarks to make on the present fashion of dressing children?

The present fashion is absurd. Children are frequently dressed like mountebanks, with feathers and furbelows and finery; the boys go bare-legged; the little girls are dressed like women, with their stuck-out petticoats, crinolines, and low dresses! Their poor little waists are drawn in tight, so that they can scarcely breathe; their dresses are very low and short, the consequence is, that a great part of the chest is exposed to our variable climate; their legs are bare down to their thin socks, or if they be clothed, they are only covered with gossamer drawers; while their feet are encased in tight shoes of paper thickness! Dress! dress! dress! is made with them, at a tender age, and when first impressions are the strongest, a most important consideration. They are thus rendered vain and frivolous.

And if they live to be women – which the present fashion is likely frequently to prevent – what are they? Silly, simpering, delicate, lack-a-daisical nonentities; dress being their amusement, their occupation, their conversation, their everything, their thoughts by day and their dreams by night! Truly they are melancholy objects to behold!

Clearly, fashion and doctors have never been comfortable companions. But it's hard to blame Chavasse for inveighing against the fashions of the day as corsets could cause permanent and irreversible damage to girls' internal organs.

~

Georgie Porgie, Pudding and Pie, Kissed the Girls and Made Them Cry ...

Play was an area where gender differences quickly became apparent. Chavasse's advice is particularly interesting because so much of it appears very modern, especially when compared to that of some of the odder twentieth-century writers like Truby King. Chavasse was anti-smacking, said Sundays should be cheerful not doleful, suggested learning through play not books and was very keen on the great outdoors. Children should always be talked to kindly, he said, and encouraged to play and be happy.

In his manual girls are not discriminated against in terms of play and exercise: there is a whole list of sports that they can take part in. He encourages them to ride, swim and dance, although some sports and activities are definitely considered for 'boys only'. But he is clearly against education for girls. He wants them to be fit and healthy because of their future roles as wives and mothers.

He ought to be encouraged to engage in those sports wherein the greatest number of muscles are brought into play. For instance, to play at ball, or hoop, or football, to play at horses, to run to certain distances and back; and, if a girl, to amuse herself with a skipping rope, such, being excellent exercise —

… A boy not partial to mischief, innocent mischief, and play, is unnatural; he is a man before his time, he is a nuisance, he is disagreeable to himself and to every one around. He is generally a sneak, and a little humbug.

… Girls, at the present time, are made clever simpletons; their brains are worked with useless knowledge, which totally unfits them for every-day duties. Their muscles are allowed to be idle, which makes them limp and flabby. The want of proper exercise ruins the complexion, and their faces become of the colour of a tallow candle! And precious wives and mothers they make when they do grow up! Grow up, did I say? They grow all manner of ways, and are as crooked as crooked sticks!

~ Clever Simpletons

It is worth while comparing the Victorian attitude to the bookish or academic child (boys as well as girls) to today's obsession with academic high-achieving at any cost. Jane Eyre mentions that had she been 'a handsome, romping, exacting child' her aunt might have loved her better: it is her very bookishness and intelligence that singles her out for blame as 'sly'. According to Chavasse, boys who are too well behaved are 'sneaks', girls who are too academic are freaks. Of course, unlike Jane Eyre, the children he wrote about were presumably future gentlemen and gentlewomen, and would not have to earn their own livings. As Becky Sharp – destined, like Jane Eyre, to be a governess – realises bitterly in *Vanity Fair*, if a woman is to live by her wits alone she has to be very clever indeed (although she was never a bluestocking, as becomes apparent soon enough in the novel: her first act is to throw Dr Johnson's Dictionary, a leaving present from her hated headmistress, out of a carriage window).

In the eighteenth century, in her *Family Book*, Hester Thrale, a friend of Dr Johnson's, describes the accomplishments of her two-year-old daughter, Queenie, whom she has trained to be an infant prodigy:

'She repeats the Pater Noster, the three Christian virtues, and the signs of the Zodiac in Watts' verses; she likewise knows them on the globe perfectly well … She knows her nine figures and the simplest combinations of them; but none beyond a hundred; "she knows all the Heathen Deities by their Attrributes and counts to 20 without missing one."'

Perhaps the Thrales, with their connections to the world of letters, were what William Thackeray would have described as 'Bohemian' and, as such, felt it was safe to encourage their children to learn. Some doctors in Victorian times believed too much study might lead to illness. This is what Thomas Bull had to say in his *The Maternal Management of Children in Infancy*:

> OVER STIMULATION
> *All causes of mental excitement should be carefully avoided, and particularly the too early or excessive exercise of the intellectual faculties. If the child be endowed with a precocious intellect, the parent must restrain rather than encourage its exercise. Nothing is more likely to light up this disease ['water on the brain'] in a constitution predisposed to it, than a premature exertion of the brain itself.*

In contrast, consider this fairly typical advertisement for children's developmental toys at www.smartbabyzone.co.uk:

> *Smart Baby Zone*
> *Smart Babies for Smart Parents*
> *Over the years studies have shown that babies learn and develop much faster when their senses are stimulated. As parents we are in constant search for toys that will ideally be fun, educational, and aid your child's mental development by stimulating their senses of vision, hearing, touch, smell and taste.*
> *Smart Baby Zone provides a range of toys that not only entertain your child but engage them to discover and explore their surrounding environment. Our range of smart products has been designed to*

be visually appealing with bright colours and to enhance your child's cognitive, creative and social development skills.

Smart Baby Zone toys have been sub-divided by age to help you choose the appropriate toy.

The assumption is that smart parents deserve smart babies (dumb babies for dumb parents, that wouldn't sell well) and that whenever possible we will buy toys that make our babies clever (mere entertainment is not enough). Look at the current vogue for baby signing:

Baby Signing – our classes can give your baby a developmental head-start.

Baby signing helps them learn to communicate before they can talk.

Baby signing – in TinyTalk classes – teaches Baby sign language – a form of pre-verbal communication.

Babies understand so much before they can talk! From as early as 6 to 9 months old, babies can begin to tell you what they want, what they are thinking about and how they feel.

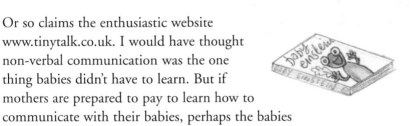

Or so claims the enthusiastic website www.tinytalk.co.uk. I would have thought non-verbal communication was the one thing babies didn't have to learn. But if mothers are prepared to pay to learn how to communicate with their babies, perhaps the babies need all the help they can get. The consumer competitive society has turned everyone into Gradgrinds, trying to turn out little geniuses who will do well at school and university, get good jobs and (eventually, when they've paid off their debts) good mortgages. We hope.

'*Play is serious business. When we see children building with blocks, pretending to be airplanes, learning to skip rope, we think, in our mixed-up, adult way, that these are just amusements, quite different from serious occupations such as doing lessons and holding a job. We are mixed up because most of us were taught in our own childhood that play was fun but that schoolwork was a duty and a job was a grind. The baby passing a rattle from one hand to the other or learning to crawl downstairs, the small boy pushing a block along a crack on the floor, pretending it's a train, are hard at work learning about the world …*'

DR SPOCK

~

When the Boys Came Out to Play, Georgie Porgie Ran Away

By the time Spock published his *Baby and Child Care* in the 1940s, play had moved on. It was no longer mere amusement or exercise. Earnest studies by psychologists, educationalists and experts of various kinds had shown just how quickly a baby developed, and how much it learnt through what looked like 'just amusements' to adult eyes. This was the new, child-centred universe, and play was 'serious business', training little girls and boys to grow up to be well-adjusted men and women (see left).

Toys had always been, to some extent, gender defined. That stalwart of the nursery, the rocking horse, was available for any child, as were the hoop, building blocks and picture books typical of the Victorian period. But elaborate dolls and dolls' houses were generally aimed at little girls, who played at overseeing the elaborate housekeeping system, with servants and a dining room, that they would perhaps one day preside over in reality. Toy soldiers, meanwhile, were aimed at boys – although the Brontë sisters in their nursery had no truck with such stereotypes. They seized the soldiers and created imaginary worlds, Gondal and Angria, for their heroes to rule and conquer. When Patrick Brontë, their father, made his children wear masks and answer questions like 'What is the difference between men and women?', it was Branwell, the soon-to-be alcoholic and ne'er-do-well son, and not his sisters, who answered: 'They differ in their minds as they do in their bodies.'

However, by the time Spock was writing, although women were wealthier, some had jobs and most had more leisure time and less housework to do thanks to the invention of gadgets and machines, they were still seen mainly as carers and home-makers, and children's toys reflected these different worlds. Girls had the stove and kitchen corner, boys had the motor car and train set:

> *A grown up playing with a child often is tempted to make the play too complicated. A mother who has bought her small daughter a doll with a whole wardrobe of clothes would like to dress the doll just right, beginning with the underclothes. But the little girl may want to start with the red overcoat ... A father who has never had enough chance to play with trains produced a whole set for his 3-year-old at Christmas. The father can't wait to get started. He fits the tracks together. But the boy has grabbed one of the cars and has shot it across the room, smack against the wall. 'No, no!' says Father. 'You put the car on the track like this.'*

Everyone has had that 'No, not like that, like this!' *Fast Show* sketch moment with their children, but I love Spock's picture of the mother wrestling with the doll's tiny underwear and the father eagerly unwrapping the train set. Notice how the toys are suited to girls or boys (although Spock does give an example of a sick boy being encouraged to colour in neatly by his mother. Perhaps it is all right for him to do this if he isn't feeling well ...). If a boy jumps the boundary, dad starts to worry:

Playing near and watching come before playing together.

> *A father may be upset if his son at 2 likes to play occasionally with dolls and doll carriages … It is perfectly natural for a regular boy of 3 or 4 to play with girls part of the time, the more so if there aren't boys of his own age available, but if they are playing house he would usually be wanting to play father or son. If a boy of 3 or 4 or 5 is avoiding boys or is regularly preferring to take the part of a mother or girl in house play, he is probably afraid of being a boy and needs child guidance help. He also needs a friendlier relationship with his father. Sometimes the mother is being too protective and enveloping.*

Paging Dr Freud! Of course, his theories dovetailed very neatly with the tendency of childcare theorists to blame everything on the mother. The mechanics of the Oedipus complex are well known, although it's not something most parents tend to think about until their son says something like 'Don't like Daddy! Hate Daddy! Want Mummy!' or their little girl starts charming her father into buying her a present. (Little girls were supposed to go through the Electra complex, but Freud never got around to explaining it very clearly.) Anyway, Oedipus clearly caused a great deal of anxiety in the world of Spock and his patients, as fathers tried to train their boys to grow up to be, well, manly men. Girls, meanwhile, could be satisfied with a compliment on their baking skills:

> *A father who wants to help his small son grow up to be manly shouldn't jump on him too hard when he cries, scorn him when he's playing a girlish game, or force him to practice athletics … A girl needs a friendly father, too … she gains confidence in herself as a girl and a woman from feeling his approval. I'm thinking of little things he can do, like complimenting her on her dress, or hair-do, or the cookies she's made.*

If Spock's approach to children's psychological development seems a little, well, unsubtle, try Jean Liedloff, author of *The Continuum Concept*, for size:

There seems to be evidence that the strong current of demand for love and attention coming from mother to son can, in its overpowering of the baby's demand, be the cause of homosexuality in his later life. The mother … often plays the role of 'little girl', and tries to beguile her child with infantile cues into paying attention to her, or feeling sorry for her. Unable to prevail against her pull on him, the child's pull on her goes unnoticed, unanswered, and he cannot free himself of his need to get her attention directed at his own loveableness. He grows up feeling that playing the pouting, flouncy little girl's role is the way to win.

Ouch! Here is Smother Mother in all her glory, turning her boy into a 'pouting, flouncy little girl'. It's hard to say who comes out of this worse – mothers, little girls or gay men. Presumably none of this funny business went on among the Yequana.

Children's Parties

Chavasse had this to say about Victorian children's parties:

One of the great follies of the present age is, children's parties, where they are allowed to be dressed up like grown-up women, stuck out in petticoats, and encouraged to eat rich cake and pastry, and to drink wine, and to sit up late at night! There is something disgusting and demoralising in all this. Their pure minds are blighted by it. Do not let me be misunderstood: there is not the least objection, but, on the contrary, great advantage, for friends' children to meet friends' children; but then let them be treated as children, and not as men and women!

I wonder what Chavasse would have made of the parties that are organised for children today – according to research by American Express parents in the United Kingdom are spending £1.4 billion on first-birthday parties (that's £450 per family). The average cost is £87, with a further £84 going on birthday presents, while 25 per cent of parents spend more than £100 on the party and 10 per cent fork out over £150. Meanwhile, presents for their child's guests cost an average of £49.

Presumably, however, there won't be any all-night wine-drinking. That's for mum and dad the night before. Birthdays seem to have shifted permanently to Saturday and Sunday mornings, as post-school get-togethers are seen as too high risk. Great for kids, but rotten for parents as they stumble through the high-decibel, brightly coloured venue yearning for a coffee, the newspaper, anything – just get me out of here ...

And, of course, the presents are all gender-coordinated. Power Rangers and Thomas for the boys, Barbie and princesses for the girls, and woe betide you if you slip the wrong gender of toy into the dreaded goodie bag.

~
Tough, Tough Toys for
Tough, Tough Boys

Liedloff's general approach to gender roles is fairly primitive, to say the least. Despite the fact that she works for a living, writing articles and giving lectures about her (one) book, as well as providing therapy from her houseboat in San Francisco, she doesn't seem to accept the idea that a woman's role goes much further than (yep) domestic duties. Here she explains how to be a good continuum-friendly mum at home – the idea is that a mother shouldn't praise a child or give it unusual attention when it behaves in a helpful or social manner, because this makes it self-conscious and will discourage it from joining in with chores:

> *Applying the principle in the easiest situation, a civilized mother would go about her domestic work with a little girl taking whatever interest she takes, but allowed to sweep with a small broom when she is inspired to do so or dust or vacuum (if she can manage the role of cleaner in her home) or help wash dishes standing on the chair.*

Back with the Yequana, meanwhile, boys have their toys and girls have – well, their manioc graters:

> *For boys, men will become the major inspiration and example in learning their part in the culture. Little girls will imitate women when their stage of development dictates that association should turn to participation. The tools will be provided if they are difficult to manufacture ... boys are provided with little bows and arrows which give valuable practice, as the arrows are straight and accurately reflect their skill ... I was present at the beginning of a little girl's working life. She was about two years old. I had seen her with the women and girls, playing as they grated manioc into a trough ... An affectionate smile and a smaller piece of manioc came from her neighbour, and her mother, ready for the inevitable impulse to show itself, handed her a tiny grating board of her own ...*

Liedloff assumes that the ability to imitate adult behaviour leads children to take on adult tasks such as childcare. Little girls (not little boys) are spoken of approvingly as taking full responsibility for babies in the Yequana tribe (so that's how the mothers dealt with the 'in arms' thing), carrying them and looking after them for hours. Boys don't do this, although they, and the men,

It worked for me

I let my children use knives from a very young age, probably about 12 months, reaching out of the sling perhaps or standing beside me helping me cook on the counter. It was just a process of observation – they really did know how to use knives because they'd seen me use them for months at that stage. And progressively they became more and more adept at using them, and more and more skilled because they obviously learn by watching. That's definitely part of the continuum concept – to allow your children to be involved in what you're doing. They observe and learn like that. *Claire, mother of two* pick up and cuddle the babies for a few minutes (cheers, mate). Their work is to practise shooting, and run about, while the girls do everything else:

> *While Yequana girls spend their childhood with other girls and women, participating from the first in their work at home or in the gardens, boys run about together most of the time [learning to shoot their arrows]; their fathers can only put their skills to real practice on suitable occasions.*

Boys are training to be Yequana patriarchs, Liedloff notes approvingly. Presumably, she herself did not have to adopt the same regimen. It's hard to imagine her sitting silently and serving the menfolk:

'It is the arrival of the father that quiets the woman and children. It is also under the eyes of the fathers and men in general that women and children take pride in doing their best, in living up to the men's expectations as well as to one another's. Boys especially like to measure themselves against their fathers, while girls enjoy serving them. It is reward enough for a little girl to be able to bring a fresh piece of cassava to her father and have him take it from her hands.'

> ## It worked for me
>
> I made a CD of songs for my son Jasper to listen to. Little boys seem to really like gay anthems and anything that's a bit 'hands in the air'. He likes 'Chasing Cars' by Snow Patrol and jazzy versions of 'Somewhere Over The Rainbow'. My CD has other stuff like 'Patience' by Take That and 'Hands Up, Baby Hands Up' and 'Daddy Cool' by Boney M – all the fathers like that one, too.
> **Carolyn, mother of Jasper (1 year)**

For much of the twentieth century, children's imitative faculties were a worry to psychologists, who believed too much baking of fairy cakes with mum at home would turn boys into fairies. The solution, clearly, was to bring in dad when he could spare his valuable time. As a result, the father's role became more important.

Mr Paterfamilias: Advice to Fathers

Even in the nineteenth century there were writers who gave advice to fathers, but it was usually on the brief side. Chavasse's main contribution (in a book in which mothers are assumed to be the teachers, doctors, nurses and moral guides to their offspring) is not to swear:

> *Let me advise you, then, Mr. Pater familias, to be careful how you converse, what language you use, while in the company of your child. Bear in mind, a child is very observant, and thinks much, weighs well, and seldom forgets all you say and all you do! Let no hasty word, then, and more especially no oath, or no impious language, ever pass your*

lips, if your child be within hearing. It is, of course, at all times wicked to swear; but it is heinously and unpardonably sinful to swear in the presence of your child! 'Childhood is like a mirror, catching and reflecting images. One impious or profane thought, uttered by a parent's lip, may operate upon the young heart like a careless spray of water thrown upon polished steel, staining it with rust, which no after scouring can efface.'

Never talk secrets before a child – 'little pitchers have long ears;' if you do, and he disclose your secrets – as most likely he will – and thus make mischief, it will be cruel to scold him; you will, for your imprudence, have yourself only to blame. Be most careful, then, in the presence of your child, of what you say, and of whom you speak.

In the early nineteenth century William Cobbett's *Advice to Young Men* included a section on fathers (see opposite). In it he suggests that rather than keeping servants a man should get his wife to do the housework until she has children. Even after his own wife had given birth they didn't have a servant for a while, because Cobbett used to help out (perhaps the first New Man?): Notice 'her' baby …

Children, and especially boys, will have some out-of-door pursuits; and it was my duty to lead them to choose such pursuits as combined future utility with present innocence. Each his flower-bed, little garden, plantation of trees; rabbits, dogs, asses, horses, pheasants and hares; hoes, spades, whips, guns; always some object of lively interest, and as much earnestness and bustle about the various objects as if our living had solely depended upon them. I made everything give way to the great object of making their lives happy and innocent.

Cobbett was a fresh-air fiend, and an advocate of cold baths, but his child-care precepts are refreshingly straightforward. Cobbett's regime of allowing his children to play with whips and guns is reminiscent of Liedloff's

'Women are all patriots of the soil; and when her neighbours used to ask my wife whether all English husbands were like hers, she boldly answered in the affirmative. I had business to occupy the whole of my time, Sundays and weekdays, except sleeping hours; but I used to make time to assist her in the taking care of her baby, and in all sorts of things: get up, light her fire, boil her tea-kettle, carry her up warm water in cold weather, take the child while she dressed herself and get the breakfast ready, then breakfast, get her in water and wood for the day, then dress myself neatly, and sally forth to my business. The moment that was over I used to hasten back to her again; and I no more thought of spending a moment away from her, unless business compelled me, than I thought of quitting the country and going to sea.'

WILLIAM COBBETT

descriptions of Yequana babies toddling about holding sharp knives by the blades, apparently unharmed. He was also a believer in home-schooling (apparently against the wishes of his wife and her friends: 'at last I answered, "I wish the boys to grow up like myself! And as for the girls, in whose hands can they be as well cared for as yours?"'):

In the meanwhile the book-learning crept in of its own accord, by imperceptible degrees. Children naturally want to be like their parents, and to do what they do: the boys following their father, and the girls their mother; and as I was always writing or reading, mine naturally desired to do something in the same way. But, at the same time, they heard no talk from fools or drinkers; saw me with no idle, gabbling, empty companions; saw no vain and affected coxcombs, and no tawdry and extravagant women; saw no nasty gormandizing; and heard no gabble about play-houses and romances and the other nonsense that fit boys to be lobby-loungers, and girls to be the ruin of industrious and frugal young men.

Cobbett's description of his home life, with his children happily reading books and playing around the kitchen table, is a lot more alluring than what is written about most Victorian schools.

Advice to fathers is non-existent in Truby King's book on babycare: dad doesn't even get a mention in the index. But by the 1940s there was a lot more anxiety over the father's role. It wasn't enough for him just to dash out to work in the morning (Cobbett, of course, was a writer and journalist, a profession well suited to home working) and come home expecting the baby to be asleep, the house immaculate and dinner on the table. Here is Gibbens on how to help a wife with her first baby:

She is bound to make mistakes, of course; who wouldn't? She has a lot to learn. It is up to you to give her every encouragement, to support her through thick and thin; and if you think things could be better done some other way, to put it tactfully … Back up your wife at all times, even if she's wrong, and tell your relatives that she's making a grand job of it, that you are proud of her and you won't have her upset … At this point you may say: 'I've got all my work cut out to make a living; the baby is her job.' But this shouldn't be so; a baby is a joint concern, and every wife appreciates a husband who shares in the upbringing of her child … Hold the baby firmly and talk to him like an intelligent being – which of course he is. Give a hand with his bath from time to time, take him on your knee and rock him up and down gently till he gurgles with laughter, play with him on the hearth rug, and if he is bottle-fed learn how to make his feeds and give him his bottle now and then. Your wife will be quick to appreciate your help and the baby will love it.

Gibbens's final comments are heart-warming:

There are no short-cuts in looking after a baby; what with feeding and cooking and washing it is a whole-time job for any woman. You may have your 40-hour week, but your wife is never free. She has hardly a moment she can call her own, especially if there are two or three children; and what with shopping, cooking, washing up, feeding and bathing the children, washing and mending their clothes, she may be working something like a 90–100 hour week … Give your wife all possible help in the house, run the baby together, see how he shapes, think over what you're going to do with him when he grows up, and you and your wife will enjoy the baby and experience some of the greatest pleasures the world has to offer you.

Compare this with the advice in *The Baby Owner's Manual,* a modern American babycare book (published in 2003) aimed at fathers:

Congratulations on the arrival of your new baby. This baby is surprisingly similar to other appliances you may already own. Like a personal computer, for instance, the baby will require a source of power to execute her many complicated tasks and functions. Like a video-cassette recorder, the baby's head will require frequent cleanings for optimum performance. And like an automobile, the baby may expel unpleasant odors into the atmosphere.

This may be jokey, but there is something rather irritating about the assumption that men will relate to babies only as consumer durables. Like the *Yummy Mummy's Survival Guide*, it plays to the stereotype (men love gadgets, women love beauty products and shopping) and applies it to parenting. Neither book is meant to be taken seriously, yet a good read of the survival guide (for research purposes, you understand) left me feeling both cross (why is it so important to be trim and toned when you've just had a baby?) and inadequate (why aren't I? Why? Why?).

Meanwhile, in the 1950s the great Dr Spock took on dad in a matey, pal-to-pal sort of way. Writers didn't condescend to fathers then, the way they might now:

A boy needs a friendly, accepting father. Boys and girls need chances to be around their father, to be enjoyed by him, and if possible, to do things with him. Unfortunately, the father is apt to come home want-ing most of all to slump down and read the paper. If he understands how valuable his companionship is, he will feel more like making a reasonable effort. I say reason-able because I don't think the conscientious father (or mother, either) should force himself beyond his endurance. Better to play for fifteen minutes enjoyably and then say, 'Now I'm going to read my paper,' than to spend all day at the zoo, crossly.

Better for whom, exactly?

Spock also suggests that bullying a son to be athletic, or being overcritical generally, may have the opposite effect to the one intended:

A boy doesn't grow up spiritually to be a man just because he's born with a male body. The thing that makes him feel and act like a man is being able to copy, to pattern himself after, men and older boys with whom he feels friendly. He can't pattern himself after a person unless he feels that this person likes him and approves of him. If a father is always impatient with or irritated with him, the boy is likely to feel uncomfortable not only when he's around his father but when he's around other men and boys, too. He is apt to draw closer to his mother and take on her manners and interests.

Uh-oh. Interestingly, both of Spock's sons said their father was rather remote, and not exactly the 'father of permissiveness' as his critics called him. They said he was a stern, if loving father.

According to the Urban Legends Reference Pages, many commentators on Spock state inaccurately that one of his sons killed himself. It was in fact his grandson, Peter, who died. As I mentioned earlier, the famous childcare expert who lost a child himself was J.B. Watson, one of whose sons, William,

'We all pretend that we find every little
nuance of our off-spring wonderful and
fascinating, but we're all lying to ourselves.
Small children are boring; it's the tedium that
dare not speak its name. I want to come out
of the closet and stand on top of the tallest
climbing frame in the counry and proclaim to
the world, "Small children are boring." All the
other parents would look shocked and offended
as they pushed their toddler up and down on
the seesaw for the one hundredth time, but
secretly they would feel a huge sense of relief
that they weren't alone. And all the guilt they
had felt because they secretly hated spending
the entire mind-numbing day with their little
two-year-olds would suddenly be lifted when
they realized that they weren't bad, unloving
parents; there was nothing wrong
with them, it was their children.
Their children were boring.'

JOHN O'FARRELL

tragically committed suicide at the age of 40. Here's a typical quote from this American behavioural psychologist, who was famous in the 1920s:

> *Mother love is a dangerous instrument. An instrument which may inflict a never healing wound … which may make infancy unhappy, adolescence a nightmare, an instrument which may wreck your adult son or daughter's vocational future and their chances for marital happiness.*

One of the most chillingly accurate depictions of modern fatherhood is in John O'Farrell's novel *The Best a Man Can Get*. Michael, the hero, is married with small children. On nights when he fancies some sleep, or just a little uninterrupted television-watching, he tells his wife he will be away on business, but instead goes to a flat where he rents a room specifically so he can be alone. Opposite he justifies his dastardly behaviour.

The book is obviously written for comic effect, but it is still uncomfortable reading for many new dads who find it hard to admit that they don't really relish sharing the parenting duties. There are probably quite a few men who would prefer a return to the good old days when all they had to do was refrain from swearing. In fact, the good old days weren't that long ago, as evidenced by this quote from an interview with a young society mother in a 1960 issue of *Mother and Baby* magazine:

> *Peter left a message with his wife that she was to say that the baby is to be brought up to respect his father! He is very proud of the fact that his method of stopping the baby crying – to dance with him to the music of the hottest jazz – is quite infallible. He is, his wife assured me, very good with the baby and will do anything for him – except change his nappies.*

There's no way nappy changing can be dodged these days.

To end this chapter you'll find a rather wonderful poem by Robert Haden about an old-fashioned father on the following page. I like the way it celebrates unselfish paternal devotion for a change:

Those Winter Sundays

Sundays too my father got up early
and put his clothes on in the blueblack cold,
then with cracked hands that ached
from labor in the weekday weather made
banked fires blaze. No one ever thanked him.

I'd wake and hear the cold splintering, breaking.
When the rooms were warm, he'd call,
and slowly I would rise and dress,
Fearing the chronic angers of that house,

Speaking indifferently to him,
who had driven out the cold
and polished my good shoes as well.
What did I know, what did I know
of love's austere and lonely offices?

ROBERT HADEN

feed baby, make dinner, answer the phone do the shopping, change baby and relax?

The Hand That Rocks The Cradle

*Any woman who is intending to go back
to work after the birth of her baby will face
all kinds of logistical and emotional problems,
but what she probably doesn't expect is a guilt
trip of Alton Towers-like proportions.*

'THE HAND THAT ROCKS THE CRADLE
Blessings on the hand of women!
Angels guard its strength and grace,
In the palace, cottage, hovel,
Oh, no matter where the place;
Would that never storms assailed it,
Rainbows ever gently curled;
For the hand that rocks the cradle
Is the hand that rules the world.'

(ABRIDGED)

~
Superwoman, Super Mum?

'You see, Katherine', Mrs Davies explained later, doing that disapproving upsneeze thing with her sinuses over teacakes, 'there are mothers who make an effort like your mum and me. And then you get the type of person who' – prolonged sniff – 'doesn't make the effort.'

Of course I knew who they were: Women Who Cut Corners. Even back in 1974, the dirty word had begun to spread about mothers who went out to work. Females who wore trouser suits and even, it was alleged, allowed their children to watch television while it was still light. Rumours of neglect clung to these creatures like dust to their pelmets.

So before I was really old enough to understand what being a woman meant, I already understood that the world of women was divided in two: there were proper mothers, self-sacrificing bakers of apple pies and well-scrubbed invigilators of the washtub, and then there were the other sort. At the age of thirty-five, I knew precisely which kind I am, and I suppose that's what I'm doing here in the small hours on the thirteenth of December, hitting mince pies with a rolling pin till they look like something mother-made. Women used to have time to make mince pies and had to fake orgasms. Now we can manage the orgasms but we have to fake the mince pies. And they call this progress.

I Don't Know How She Does It by Allison Pearson struck a chord with many working mothers. The story of Kate, the high-flying City woman with two small children, an indolent cleaner and a List of Things To Do as long as your arm, resonated with a lot of women who were fed up with reading reports about children of working mothers performing badly in school, or being more aggressive, or more prone to depression, when all they were trying to do was pay the mortgage and help support their families … I Googled 'Working mothers UK' and got the following results, and if you do the same you'll probably get something similar:

Mother at Work (webzine for working mothers)

The impact of mothers' employment on family relationships (the proportion of working mothers with dependent children is increasing) – BBC News

Mothers, work and the guilt factor (Lisa, working mother of one, with another on the way!) – BBC News

UK working mothers earn less

Working mothers get the blame – iVillage (working mothers are in the firing line again, reports Lauren Booth)

Official; babies do best with mother – the Observer (one of the longest and most detailed studies of UK childcare has concluded … and 78 per cent of working mothers say a nursery is their 'ideal childcare')

Working mothers 'damage their child's health'

Emergency childcare for working mothers – Guardian Unlimited (working mothers are to be offered 'emergency childcare')

Boost pay to help working mothers, says Harman

Of these nine search results, six are negative about working mothers, two positive and one neutral. And the search results should reflect fairly accurately the coverage the subject gets in the media. It just goes to show the torrent of negative information working mothers face.

Even working part-time carries its own penalties. You may escape being seen as a hard-nosed, child-neglecting career bitch, but after just one year your earnings will suffer for a staggering 15 years, according to the Equal Opportunities Commission whose studies on this subject make illuminating reading:

'Part-time work has a "scarring effect" on earnings. The longer a person is in part-time work, the lower their wages are likely to be, even if they return to full-time work. Women who have spent just one year in part-time work, and then work full-time, can still expect to earn 10% less after 15 years than those who worked full time for the same period.'

Spock's Working Mother

By 1957, Dr Spock had realised that some women work and had a whole section devoted to them in *Baby and Child Care* (in the Special Problems chapter). It makes interesting reading:

A few mothers, particularly those with professional training, feel that they must work because they wouldn't be happy otherwise. I wouldn't disagree if a mother felt strongly about it, provided she had an ideal arrangement for her children's care. After all, an unhappy mother can't bring up very happy children.

What about the mothers who don't absolutely have to work but would prefer to, either to supplement the family income or because they think they will be more satisfied and therefore get along better at home? That's harder to answer ... If a mother realizes clearly how vital this kind of care is to a small child, it may make it easier for her to decide that the extra

money she might earn, or the satisfaction she might receive from an outside job, is not so important, after all.

A day nursery or a 'baby farm' is no good for an infant. There's nowhere near enough attention or affection to go around ...

The infant whose mother can't take care of him during the daytime needs individual care, whether it's in his own home or someone else's.

In other words, a baby should not have to put up with second best. However permissive Spock may have seemed to right-wingers, for him a woman's place was still very much firmly in the home.

In 2005 a study for the RAC Foundation UK found that what most mothers wanted for Mother's Day was a chance to spend more time with their families:

* Over 70% of working mothers in the UK would like to work flexibly or telework at least some of the week.
* Women now work half a day longer than five years ago – an average of almost 34 hours a week.
* A quarter of working mothers said that the UK's long hours' culture had a detrimental affect on their mental health, their relationship with children and their sex lives.
* Asked what they would like for Mother's Day more than six out of ten asked for more time to spend with families.

Like the evasive first-time mother in *In the Fold* by Rachel Cusk, who slowly edges away from her husband and baby, and becomes more and more immersed in her career until she is finally completely estranged from them apart from an occasional visit to the former family home, we're withdrawing from our partners and even our children under the strain of reconciling our different roles.

The Loneliness of the Long-distance Mother

At the same time, what are now known as 'stay-at-home mums' are writing more and more about the difficulty of their lot. When you give up work to look after your children full-time you might discover that you sacrifice your career, financial security and even your mental health – as well as your status in a society that values worker bees more than queen bees.

An article in the *Observer* looked at female stereotypes (earth mother, superwoman, yummy mummy, and so on). Rather than peddle the standard 'earth mother' line about how fulfilling it is to be at home all day with her children, one of the interviewees said honestly that she was starting to feel fed up:

Nikki Zanchi, 43:
Lives in Somerset with her husband and children, Fabia, 19, Grace, 11, Esme, 9, Ruby, 6, and Eli, 2.
Mothering happens over many, many years. It's a struggle and no one should preach about how to do it. I do firmly believe that breast milk is the best milk in the world, but I don't think that doing it for a long time necessarily makes someone a better mother. I only breast-fed my eldest daughter for two months because I was a single mother then and had to go back to work. It broke my heart. Meanwhile, I've given my other four

children my life's blood. I've slept with them, carried them, breast-fed them for years, home schooled them, and to be honest I'm knackered. I want to move on from birthing now. I want to move into my life. I want my kids to see that women do things. I know being a full-time mother is the hardest job in the world, and I'm so proud of my kids, but sometimes I feel as if my life is slipping away. Being at home with the kids full time involves quite a lot of sacrifice.
(14 JANUARY 2007)

There's a new trendiness about the role of the stay-at-home mum (as presented in the media) that the suburban heroines of *The Women's Room*, the late 1950s feminist best-seller in the United States, desperate to escape from their household drudgery, overbearing husbands and demanding kids, would never have recognised. Take Jools Oliver, for example, the beautiful wife of Jamie Oliver, mother of two and most recently author of *Zero to Nine; the Diary of an Honest Mum*. She and Jamie were voted the celebrities most British parents would turn to for advice (after Richard and Judy!). Her description of parenting is certainly one any mother would recognise:

Prologue
So here I am on my knees surrounded by antibacterial wipes, disinfectant spray and POO! ... Once again my youngest daughter, Daisy, has decided to cover herself in her poo. This has been happening on a regular basis for the last few weeks. She decides to wait until she is inside her freshly laundered Grobag, in her pristine white cot, surrounded with toys and books, during her lunchtime nap. And then she poos. And then she gets it EVERYWHERE, usually decorating her cot with it. I generally never make it in time to catch her. I walk into her room and see her cheeky smile as she shows off her artistic abilities and invites me to join in!

Today it doesn't seem at all funny though. I am a bit ticked off as I see that she has done it yet again. I'm tired. We've just moved to a new house and the place is full of builders, plumbers and engineers. All I can hear are drills and the pounding of the radio, and I've got a headache. We're now going to be very late for Poppy's ballet class and on top of all this the plumbers have turned off the water and electricity … arghhhhhhh!

baby yoga

It worked for me

One thing that really worked for me was to set up a time (mine was 10 a.m.) to pump milk each day. I only spent 15 minutes on the project, so I only got a few ounces, but if you do it at the same time each day, it adds up. Then, when you want to go on a date or have an important meeting – no worries!

Something that works well for working moms is to put their office clothes on then wear a robe or house dress over them. That way, they can get messy and burped on but, take off that smeary robe just before leaving the house and – voila! – clean mommy! *Anna, mother of Hank (6 years) and Jonathon (2 years)*

And yet ... Can celebrity stay-at-home-mothers, with their ready access to help, money and power, really be the best role models to follow? Isn't donning even an ironic, part-time pinny, like Nigella Lawson, the Domestic Goddess, a step backwards? What is interesting is that so many of the mothers selling us this retro, Cath Kidston-style vision of happy faces round the kitchen table are career women too, able to balance children and work as authors (like Jools or Nigella) or running websites, writing articles or publishing magazines. The original superwoman, Shirley Conran, famously said that 'Life is too short to stuff a mushroom', and that she'd rather lie on a sofa than sweep under it, but nowadays it seems that women are expected to have careers, look after their children as much as possible *and* be good housewives! No wonder something sometimes has to give. This is what Jerry Hall has to say on the subject:

'My mother said keeping a man is simple: you must be a maid in the living room, a cook in the kitchen and a whore in the bedroom. I said I'd hire the other two and take care of the bedroom bit myself.'

Nowadays, we're more likely to be hiring a divorce lawyer after finding that we're too knackered by all the demands on our time to cope with the 'bedroom bit'. The nookie crisis among parents in the United States has reached such proportions it has generated its own sexpert, Esther Perel, author of *Mating in Captivity*:

There's a powerful tendency in long-term relationships to favour the predictable over the unpredictable. Yet without an element of uncertainty there is no longing, no anticipation, no frisson.

Perel's tips include stopping breastfeeding (the hormones disrupt your libido), and going on a yearly holiday with your spouse and without your baby (great if you can afford the childcare). It sounds as though typical motherhood is a bit incompatible with being sexy, as far as she is concerned.

Green and eco-friendly philosophies, as well as attachment theory, bring with them issues about a mother's role in particular. If you decide on eco-nappies, grow your own vegetables, eschew the dishwasher and washing machine and wash everything by hand (as my mother did for years, as well as making her own yoghurt, preserves, etc.), and are with your children most of the time (probably with no television in the house) how on earth are you going to find time to work? Being an eco-mother is a full-time job ...

Attachment theory also assumes that the 'natural', and best, way to look after babies in the modern world is to be with them all the time. In this extract from *The Continuum Concept* Jean Liedloff describes how to do the housework with an in-arms baby. (I've done it with my baby in a sling, but not terribly well, or quickly, and certainly not while simultaneously holding down a job.)

Holding a baby while doing housework is a matter of skill. A sling over one shoulder which supports the baby on the opposite hip is helpful. Dusting and vacuum-cleaning can be done mainly with one hand. Bed-making will be a little more difficult, but a resourceful mother will find a way to do it. Cooking is largely a matter of keeping one's body between the stove and the baby when there is danger of splashing. Dishwashing can be done with one hand if necessary, but often there will be someone there to hold the baby while its mother is doing it.

'Put the baby dooown!' I find myself crying to the imaginary mother in this scenario. And in fact, in Liedloff world, this is exactly what happened: the child was palmed off on a passing small girl, or fellow tribeswoman, or just plonked down next to a large pit for a bit of continuum-style free play. Otherwise it's hard to see how the women got the gardening, cooking and everything else done before their menfolk came back from a long day shooting arrows (yes, of course hunting is hard work, one imagines a Yequana wife moaning, but I've been doing this babe-in-arms stuff all day long! He has no idea!).

Attachment theorists don't always make it clear that 'full-time' mothering needn't mean twenty-four/seven. Like Penelope Leach in *Who Cares?*, they stress continuity of care, and the ability to give the baby a lot of attention.

How and Why Changing Caregivers Damage a Young Child
A baby who does not have anybody special, but is cared for by many well-meaning strangers in turn, or one who is cared for sketchily and without concentration, sharing his caretaker with other needful small people, is like an adult who moves from country to country, knowing the language of none.

... If the strangers are part- or full-time substitute parents who, once on the scene, remain constantly part of his life, he will gradually adapt. If his mother is around to help him make the transition, to 'translate him' for the newcomers and to blend their 'style' with her own, he will adapt more quickly. The new people will be made 'special'. He will teach them to understand him and to respond to him just as he taught his mother. But if the newcomers to his life have no time to 'listen' to him, concentrate on him, feel their way with him, perhaps because he is now

part of a group or perhaps because they are part of a stream of short-term caretakers, his development may truly suffer ... '

Heart-rending stuff – unless, of course, you are a government minister trying to solve the problem of child poverty by persuading single mothers to go out to work. It might might very well be argued that attachment theory is something of a middle-class luxury.

Whose Hand Rocks the Cradle?

Mother–baby bonding is a relatively modern preoccupation. As we have seen, in the late eighteenth and early nineteenth centuries it was customary for the upper- and middle-classes to have servants, and babies were often sent away 'to nurse'. In his *Advice to Young Men*, the early nineteenth-century radical William Cobbett was one of the first people to speak out against wet nursing. He did not approve of servants in general, but also objected to the

custom because of a surprisingly modern concern that the baby would
bond with the nurse rather than its mother, and because wet nurses not
infrequently abandoned their own babies in order to suckle someone else's
(see opposite).

The vexed question of 'help' has always been an issue. Nowadays only 1 per
cent of families with small children in the United Kingdom has a nanny or au
pair, but these childcarers have a mystique, and a fascination, that is reflected
in the tabloids and on television. From the bonkable au pair to the nightmare
nanny, stereotypes in the media suggest that mothers have to be constantly on
the alert. Jude Law's was probably the archetypal 'naughty nanny', servicing
the lord and master as well as his brood. The alternative stereotype is the
reassuring, starchy, sexless yet quasi-maternal figure of the Victorian and
Edwardian nanny, the one we associate with Mary Poppins and wish we had
at home instead of our fallible selves.

By the mid-nineteenth century, the population explosion in the middle
and lower classes had brought the two together in the same house, 'above'
and 'below' stairs. In Mrs Beeton's world, the structure of a household was
reassuringly well organised and rigidly hierarchical. The nursemaid, or upper
nursemaid, ruled the nursery. If a family had enough money, they also had
an under-nursemaid to help out. Mrs Beeton, who is generally thought of
as a stalwart Victorian matriarch, was only 29 when she died. She gave birth
to four children, two of whom were tragically lost to sickness, so when she
gives advice about nurses, childhood illnesses and nurseries in her *Book of
Household Management* she is clearly drawing on her own experience:

> *Upper and Under Nursemaids.*
> *The nursery is of great importance in every family, and in families of
> distinction, where there are several young children, it is an establishment
> kept apart from the rest of the family, under the charge of an upper nurse,
> assisted by under nursery-maids proportioned to the work to be done.
> The responsible duties of upper nursemaid commence with the weaning
> of the child: it must now be separated from the mother or wet-nurse, at*

'I had the pleasure to know, in Hampshire, a lady who had brought up a family of ten children by hand, as they call it [artificial feeding]. Owing to some defect, she could not suckle her children; but she wisely and heroically resolved, that her children should hang upon no other breast, and that she would not participate in the crime of robbing another child of its birthright, and, as is mostly the case, of its life. Who has not seen these banished children, when brought and put into the arms of their mothers, screaming to get from them, and stretch out their little hands to get back into the arms of the nurse, and when safely got there, hugging the hireling as if her bosom were a place of refuge? Why, such a sight is, one would think, enough to strike a mother dead. And what sort of a husband and father, I want to know, must that be, who can endure the thought of his child loving another woman more than its own mother and his wife?'

WILLIAM COBBETT

least for a time, and the cares of the nursemaid, which have hitherto been only occasionally put in requisition, are now to be entirely devoted to the infant. She washes, dresses, and feeds it; walks out with it, and regulates all its little wants; and, even at this early age, many good qualities are required to do so in a satisfactory manner. Patience and good temper are indispensable qualities; truthfulness, purity of manners, minute cleanliness, and docility and obedience, almost equally so. She ought also to be acquainted with the art of ironing and trimming little caps, and be handy with her needle.

The responsibilities of the upper nursemaid did not end there. She was also supposed to be a moral guide, training the children in both discipline and manners. Notice how Mrs Beeton talks about punishing and bribing children: clearly these were already preoccupations for parents.

Most children have some bad habit, of which they must be broken; but this is never accomplished by harshness without developing worse evils: kindness, perseverance, and patience in the nurse, are here of the utmost importance. When finger-sucking is one of these habits, the fingers are sometimes rubbed with bitter aloes, or some equally disagreeable substance. Others have dirty habits, which are only to be changed by patience, perseverance, and, above all, by regularity in the nurse. She should never be permitted to inflict punishment on these occasions, or, indeed, on any occasion. But, if punishment is to be avoided, it is still more necessary that all kinds of indulgences and flattery be equally forbidden ... A child should never be led to think others inferior to it, to beat a dog, or even the stone against which it falls, as some children are taught to do by silly nurses. Neither should the nurse affect or show alarm at any of the little accidents which must inevitably happen: if it falls, treat it as a trifle; otherwise she encourages a spirit of cowardice and timidity. But she will take care that such accidents are not of frequent occurrence, or the result of neglect.

Cleanliness was also important, although Mrs Beeton did not want her children dressed up like little dolls:

The nurse should keep the child as clean as possible, and particularly she should train it to habits of cleanliness, so that it should feel uncomfortable when otherwise; watching especially that it does not soil itself in eating. At the same time, vanity in its personal appearance is not to be encouraged by over-care in this respect, or by too tight lacing or buttoning of dresses, nor a small foot cultivated by the use of tight shoes.

Mrs Beeton had another modern preoccupation, or one we think of as modern, following the invention of 'nannycams' hidden inside the child's nursery. Could the nanny be trusted? Was the nanny informing the parents of everything important? Was she missing things out? In her book she writes about nurses and wet nurses dosing their little charges, or not informing the mother when they were unwell. Clearly, the safety of her children was a worry to the Victorian mum:

Nursemaids would do well to repeat to the parents faithfully and truly the defects they observe in the dispositions of very young children. If properly checked in time, evil propensities may be eradicated; but this should not extend to anything but serious defects; otherwise, the intuitive perceptions which all children possess will construe the act into 'spying' and 'informing', which should never be resorted to in the case of children, nor, indeed, in any case.

Finally, these are the tasks of a nursemaid's assistant, an under-nursemaid, who might be employed in wealthier households to help with the heavy work – and it was heavy, in the days before plumbing, washing machines or central heating:

> *Such are the cares which devolve upon the nursemaid, and it is her duty to fulfil them personally. In large establishments she will have assistants proportioned to the number of children of which she has the care. The under nursemaid lights the fires, sweeps, scours, and dusts the rooms, and makes the beds; empties slops, and carries up water; brings up and removes the nursery meals; washes and dresses all the children, except the infant, and assists in mending. Where there is a nursery girl to assist, she does the rougher part of the cleaning; and all take their meals in the nursery together, after the children of the family have done.*

For all this work, nursemaids could expect the handsome annual remuneration detailed below:

	When no extra allowance is made for Tea, Sugar, and Beer.	When an extra allowance is made for Tea, Sugar, and Beer.
The Head Nurse	£15 to 30	£13 to 26
The Nursemaid	£8 to 12	£5 to 10

A Spoonful of Sugar

When *Mary Poppins* by P.L. Travers was published in 1934, and even in 1902, the time of *Peter Pan* by J.M. Barrie, this tightly ordered world was disintegrating. According to Barrie's stage directions for the theatrical version of the book, which was first performed in 1904, the Darling family live in a strapped-for-cash household in 'a depressed street in Bloomsbury', where the one maid, Liza, is referred to as 'the servants' and Nanny is Nana, a dog. Why is Nana a dog? Again, I quote the stage directions for the play:

> *The only occupant of the room at present is Nana the nurse, reclining, not as you might expect on the one soft chair, but on the floor. She is a Newfoundland dog, and though this may shock the grandiose, the not exactly affluent will make allowances. The Darlings could not afford to have a nurse, they could not afford indeed to have children; and now you are beginning to understand how they did it. Of course Nana has been trained by Mrs. Darling, but like all treasures she was born to it. In this play we shall see her chiefly inside the house, but she was just as exemplary outside, escorting the two elders to school with an umbrella in her mouth, for instance, and butting them back into line if they strayed.*

The Darlings were the victims of a problem familiar to modern parents: they simply couldn't afford any help. However, as we know, when Mr Darling foolishly prevents Nana doing her job disaster strikes and Peter Pan lures all three children away from the nursery, leaving their mother and father distraught. It's one of the first examples in fiction of a parent–nanny conflict, in the familiar context of stressed parents about to go out for the evening. Mr Darling, who has a slightly sadistic sense of humour, puts medicine in Nana's bowl instead of her drink, and a family row develops. This is an extract from the book:

Mrs Darling smelt the bowl. 'O George,' she said, 'it's your medicine!'

'It was only a joke,' he roared, while she comforted her boys, and Wendy hugged Nana. 'Much good,' he said bitterly, 'my wearing myself to the bone trying to be funny in this house.'

And still Wendy hugged Nana. 'That's right,' he shouted. 'Coddle her! Nobody coddles me. Oh dear no! I am only the breadwinner, why should I be coddled, why, why, why!'

'George,' Mrs Darling entreated him, 'not so loud; the servants will hear you.' Somehow they had got into the way of calling Liza the servants.

'Let them,' he answered recklessly. 'Bring in the whole world. But I refuse to allow that dog to lord it in my nursery for an hour longer.'

The children wept, and Nana ran to him beseechingly, but he waved her back. He felt he was a strong man again. 'In vain, in vain,' he cried; 'the proper place for you is the yard, and there you go to be tied up this instant.'

The start of *Mary Poppins* is equally bizarre. The nanny arrives in a storm, bullies Mrs Banks (who, like the Darlings, lives in straitened circumstances, in 'the smallest house in the Lane') into giving her a job, rushes off to the nursery and doses the children with a mysterious medicine:

Then, with a long, loud sniff, that seemed to indicate that she had made up her mind, she said; 'I'll take the position.' 'For all the world,' as Mrs Banks said to her husband later, 'as though she were doing us an honour.'

At the age of ten P.L. Travers had been left in charge of her two siblings when their mother ran off into a thunderstorm saying she was going to kill herself. The little girl lay on a hearthrug and told the children stories until the mother returned, having changed her mind. In *Mary Poppins* there is an enduring preoccupation with the safety of children, and the reliability (or not) of the person who looks after them. Mary Poppins is an ambiguous figure, sometimes scary, sometimes bossy. However, the children adore her, and when she leaves 'when the wind changes', as she had told them she would, they are heartbroken. When Michael tells his mother he loves Mary Poppins most in the world, she is more preoccupied with who is to look after the children than worried that her rightful place has been usurped. Emotional upheaval is less important than practical upheaval. In the film, which is, of course, a Disneyfication of the original book, Mrs Banks gives up her work (as a suffragette) and looks after the children herself.

Top Nanny Movies

Sound of Music: Julie Andrews is the ultimate au pair.

Mary Poppins: Julie Andrews sings and she can wiggle her nose. What more could a child want?

Nanny McPhee: Emma Thompson does Mary Poppins with warts on.

Mrs Doubtfire: Robin Williams is much more palatable as Mrs Doubtfire than as deadbeat dad.

Jack and Sarah: Widower Richard E. Grant hires an American waitress (Samantha Mathis) as a nanny. She knows nothing about looking after children but does wonders for bereaved husbands.

The Hand that Rocks the Cradle: Rebecca de Mornay is the ultimate anti-nanny. Don't watch this if you're about to go back to work.

~
Who Stays at Home?

Most modern parents, especially mothers, feel torn when they can't be at home to comfort a sick or injured child, or when work and domestic worlds collide. The following was posted by Eleanor Mills on the working mother blog www.alphamummy.com:

> *Occasionally, even in the best run households (and I wouldn't claim to have one of those) you get a real childcare crisis. Try this one for size: I had a crucial meeting but my nanny was in Slovakia (her father died), my husband's firm had just been taken over by a new company so he had to be there, my mum was in Mozambique (lucky cow but that's another story), my sister (who can do it at a pinch) was in Wales, the cleaner was at her daughter's, the old nanny who covers for us sometimes was at work. Help. What is a working mummy supposed to do? After all no one's boss will go for 'I've got no child care I can't make it' but sometimes that really is the truth. I toyed with pulling a sickie (impossible – you've got to be dying not to go into my office). And then I begged and begged and begged my husband to do it. He did. But the downside was massive. A furious, resentful husband. Not a pretty sight. But it got me thinking – hey mums out there, when there is a pinch, who gives in in your house-hold? It's all about who has the most important job and that's not a fault line any of us want to scrutinise too closely.*

Even Mrs X, the ghastly society matron in *The Nanny Diaries*, the best-selling New York roman-à-clef, flinches when her child Grayer runs to the nanny rather than her when he hurts himself and ends up sacking Nan. The book is the classic nightmare-mum story, told from the point of view of the nanny, whose employer doesn't work, clean, cook or look after her child, but requires constant assistance from her large staff. Nan describes, for example, how

Mrs X expects her to deal with the emotional and practical consequences when her son is sick:

I hit the mattress with my hand and roll onto my back. Staring up at the Xes' guest-room ceiling, I try to add up the few hours of sleep I've managed to get in the past three nights and the total makes me even heavier. I'm bone tired from spending twenty-four/seven keeping Grayer entertained as his mood has blackened and fever risen.

When I arrived she greeted me at the elevator with a list in her hand, her bags already waiting in the limo downstairs. She just wanted to 'mention' that Grayer had a 'tiny bit of an earache' and that his medicine was by the sink, along with his pediatrician's number – 'just in case'. And the kicker: 'We really prefer that Grayer not sit in front of the television. You two have fun!'

I knew fun was hardly going to be the word for it as soon as I found him lying on the floor next to his train set, listlessly rolling a caboose on his arm.

It worked for me

I have had nannies and au pairs for about 15 years now and I have a few rules: Do pay top whack – childcare is exhausting and often mind-numbing. Value your childcarer and she will pass that on to your kids. Do look for fluent English. A good command of English is essential – carers who are learning English are fine so long as they are not in sole charge. You will never have peace of mind if the only way to communicate with your nanny in an emergency is through an interpreter. Don't be jealous – your children will always love you best. No matter what. So be pleased if your children adore the nanny; think how awful it would be if they didn't. Don't have doubts. If you think your nanny isn't up to scratch, talk to her about your misgivings and, if she doesn't assuage your fears, find someone else. There is nothing worse for mother or child than an atmosphere of mutual distrust. ***Amanda, mother of four***

The text on the back of the book sums up what the advertisement for Nan's job should have said:

'WANTED One young woman to take care of four-year-old boy. Must be cheerful, enthusiastic, and selfless-bordering-on-masochistic. Must relish sixteen-hour shifts with a deliberately nap-deprived preschooler. Must love getting thrown up on, literally and figuratively, by everyone in his family. Must enjoy the delicious anticipation of ridiculously erratic pay. Mostly, must love being treated like fungus found growing out of employer's Hermés Bag. Those who take it personally need not apply.'

The relationship between parents and childcarer is always, in the end, personal, and can be fraught. No matter how starchy the nanny, or unflappable the Australian au pair, there is always the question: is this the best care my child can get? Is it (God forbid) better than it gets from me? In the nineteenth century, just as today, there was concern about nannies being careless with their charges, as Dr Michael Underwood made clear in his *Diseases of Children*. If they weren't flirting with soldiers (and allowing them to kiss the babies) or dosing their charges with opium, they were leaving them in draughts:

Much caution, indeed, is necessary on this head in this unsettled climate, and envinces the necessity of parents superintending those to whose care they intrust infant children, since nurserymaids are often indiscreet in keeping them too long in the air at a time, which is a frequent occasion of their taking cold, and deters many parents from sending them abroad as often as they should. Another, and a worse, as well as a common fault of nurses and servants, is that of standing still, with children in their arms, in a current of air, or either sitting down with other servants, and suffering children who can run about, to play at a little distance by themselves; to sit down on the grass, or in damp places, and such like irregularities; the consequences of which are often a long confinement to a warm room, and either a prohibition against going out so much as they ought, or a fresh cold, owing to a repetition of such irregularities.

What About Dad?

Why not let men do the mothering? The argument is so fatuous it deserves all the banality of the response: because they are men. If in the 100,000 years of human development men had taken over the traditional feminine role, I would say, yes, why not? If you suggest that we have changed men so radically over the past twenty years that they now go completely against type, culture and tradition, then you are deluded. The 'new man', like the glamorous career women, is an invention of the industry that feeds upon the insecurities of women.

In the United Kingdom men work the longest hours in Europe, and recently there has been a lot of hand-wringing over this fact and the effect it may well be having on British families. Despite these long hours – and statements like the quote above, from Paula Yates's *The Fun Starts Here: A Practical Guide to the Bliss of Babies* – 30 per cent of children with working mothers are looked after by their fathers.

According to the Equal Opportunities Commission in its Facts About Dads Today policy statement:

> *Fathers are spending more time with their children: in the late 1990s, fathers of children under 5 were spending an average two hours a day on child-related activities, compared to less than a quarter of an hour per day in the mid 1970s.*
>
> *Fathers' time spent with their children accounts for one third of total parental childcare time.*
>
> *Where mothers work, one third cite fathers as the main child carer while they are at work.*

However, opinions like Paula Yates's are still pretty much routine. We criticise men for not taking over more childcare, and we criticise them when they do. Yet some women have adjusted to letting their husbands do the hard work. An example is Helena Morrissey, whose husband is a Buddhist monk and full-time carer to their eight children, and who was interviewed for the *Observer* article about female sterotypes:

> *Superwomen*
> *Helena Morrissey, 40: CEO of Newton Fund Management Company, which manages in excess of £32.8 billion. Lives in London with her husband and their seven children. Expecting her eighth.*
>
> *The word super implies that you have superhuman tendencies and it's not like that. There is no magic formula. I wouldn't say that I have a masochistic streak, but it has been suggested sometimes. What I do have is a high appetite for hard work. I feel lucky to have lots of children and a fulfilling career and not to have had to choose one or the other. I have a truly marvellous husband who stays at home and helps with the children. I believe very strongly in the continuum concept – which means that your baby is on you all the time, so although my maternity leaves are*

*short, they are intense. Then it's a gradual handover to my husband —
and we have a nanny — when I go back to work. We didn't envisage
having eight children, but in fact it's easier now than when we had our
first. I was 25 then and we were both working and running to and from
the nursery.*

It worked for me

We still find childcare quite difficult as Mark and I both have to work flexible
schedules. Mark helps me out though, and vice versa. At first I was nervous
about Jasper being alone a lot with his dad, because I felt Mark could be quite
slapdash and I'm a bit of a control freak. Now I'm much more relaxed about it.
But you do have to teach dads how to deal with things like bottles! *Carolyn,
mother of Jasper (1 year)*

~ ... *And Grandparents?*

And finally ... grandparents. In desperation, many modern working parents turn to their own mothers and fathers to answer the conundrum of who is left holding the baby. In fact, 27 per cent of babies whose mothers work are looked after by their grandparents (which means that 57 per cent of children with working mothers are looked after by either their father or their grandparents).

Nevertheless, in an FCCC (Families, Children and Childcare) study Penelope Leach, a grandmother herself, found that grandparents were not necessarily any better for children than nannies or childminders:

> *The quality of care offered in four different types of non-maternal child care to 307 infants at 10 months and 331 infants at eighteen months old was compared and factors associated with higher quality were identified. Observed quality was lowest in nurseries, except that at eighteen months they offered more learning activities. There were few differences in the observed quality of care by child minders, grandparents and nannies, although grandparents had somewhat lower safety and health scores and offered children fewer activities. Cost was largely unrelated to quality of care except in child minding where higher costs were associated with higher quality. Observed ratios of children to adults had a significant impact on quality of nursery care; the more infants each adult had to care for the lower the quality of the care she gave them. Mothers' overall satisfaction with their child's care was positively associated with its quality for home-based care but not for nursery settings.*

In an interview in the *Guardian*, Miriam Stoppard, a guru who is also a grandmother, spoke beautifully about the joys of having grandchildren:

'The wonderful thing is that grandchildren pull you into their world, you're on the same level and you can introduce your grandchildren to rare possibilities. Parents have so many domestic pressures: they're worried about money, jobs. A grandparent has a bigger menu to draw on. Your children may appreciate all the help you give them, but your little grandchildren want to show you everything because they know you're a guaranteed source of praise. I always say "I'm proud of you," then they feel they're in the spotlight and they feel on top of the world. I feel that I've been put on earth to love my grandchildren. Your grandchildren can be a love object in a way that your own children can't. You eat, sleep and breathe your own children. They're just too close to you. They're part of your life. You're doing the school runs, getting the football kit ready, whatever. But with a grandchild one has the space to fall in love.'

(4 November 2006)

It worked for me

I'm currently living in the same house as my mother so she helps out when I'm feeling overwhelmed, and will take Max for a while so I can do the housework or have a shower. If we put the baby monitor on for her, we can go out in the evening for a drink or meet up with friends. My partner Jamie's mother will also sometimes take care of him overnight or for a day to give me a break. It's a great help, now that I'm thinking of setting up my own business. *Chloe, mother of Max (1 year)*

Miriam Stoppard sounds like the ideal grandmother. Unfortunately, many grandparents, although doting, can be infuriatingly busy with their Saga cruises and grown-up gap years. Furthermore, as the FCCC study says, while they are more trusted than younger caregivers they tend to provide less stimulation.

In the end, whether you go back to work or stay at home, someone will make you feel guilty about your choice. But if you've read this book you will know that all advice about childcare is ultimately subjective. One expert's controlled crying is another's controlled cruelty. The 'in arms' method of childrearing is heaven for some and a ball and chain for others. Even something as seemingly innocuous as the kind of pushchair to buy is a thorny ideological issue: should it face forwards to foster independence or backwards to promote the mother–baby attachment? When reading any childcare book it's worth remembering that the author wants your soul and probably your

It worked for me

My mother comes to look after Rory and Ben two days a week so I can go to work. I pay her to help me out but in fact the work she does is priceless, because I have complete peace of mind knowing they are with her. *Elizabeth, mother of Rory (4 years) and Ben (1 year)*

wallet as well. No one wrote a best-selling manual by being wishy-washy. Readers are looking for certainties, and that's what they get – even if those certainties can be diametrically opposed.

I think childcare manuals are invaluable when your baby wakes up in the night covered in red spots, or if you need support when your mother-in-law starts wondering aloud if baby hasn't yet started on solids. They are great for back-up and reference, and as interesting pieces of social history, but they are not holy writ. While it is tempting to feel they might have the answers in the wee small hours of the morning when your baby just won't go back to sleep, the inconvenient truth is that the only childcare regimen you can follow with conviction is your own.

No one gets parenting right, as Philip Larkin points out in 'This Be the Verse' (They fuck you up your mum and dad/ they may not mean to but they do), so relax in the knowledge that all you can do is your best. And remember that the hardest thing of all isn't knowing what to do – it's knowing when to do nothing. I particularly like the poem by Cecil Day-Lewis on the following page about the moment every parent faces, when their child walks away from them and their job is to let it go.

Walking Away

It is eighteen years ago, almost to the day –
a sunny day with the leaves just turning,
The touch-lines new-ruled – since I watched you play
Your first game of football, then, like a satellite
Wrenched from its orbit, go drifting away

Behind a scatter of boys. I can see
You walking away from me towards the school
With the pathos of a half-fledged thing set free
Into a wildness, the gait of one
Who finds no path where the path should be.

That hesitant figure, eddying away
Like a winged seed loosened from its parent stem,
Has something I never quite grasp to convey
About nature's give-and-take – the small, the scorching
Ordeals which fire one's irresolute clay.

I have had worse partings, but none that so
Gnaws at my mind still. Perhaps it is roughly
Saying what God alone could perfectly show –
How selfhood begins with a walking away.
And love is proved in the letting go.

CECIL DAY-LEWIS

~ *Acknowledgements*

I wrote this book with the help of my sister Tabitha who, like me, has two children and an overstocked library of baby books. She did so much hard work despite the two aforesaid children and I am deeply grateful to her for giving this book substance.

I should also thank Anna Davies and Tanya Shaw, the producers of the accompanying television series, Hamish Mykura and David Glover at Channel 4, and Rowena Webb and Sarah Reece at Hodder & Stoughton.

And, of course, thanks to all the mums and dads – both on www.net-mums.com and in the flesh – who answered our questions, contributed their experiences and told us their top parenting tips!

~
Picture Credits

Hodder & Stoughton would like to thank the following for providing photographs and illustrations and for permission to reproduce copyright material.

Page 24 *Feeding and Care of Baby* by Truby King, 1937; 42 *The Common Sense Book of Baby and Child Care* by Dr Benjamin Spock, 1945, illustrations by Dorothea Fox; 56 'American Feeding Bottles' by T.G. Drake, *Journal of the History of Medicine*; 93 Wellcome Trust Photo Library; 128, 130 and 135 Getty Images; 177 and 181 *Feeding and Care of Baby* by Truby King, 1937; 188 and 200 *The Care of Young Babies* by John Gibbens, 1940; 205 *The Mothercraft Manual* by Mabel Liddiard, 1948; 208 and 234 *The Common Sense Book of Baby and Child Care* by Dr Benjamin Spock, 1945, illustrations by Dorothea Fox; 258 and 267 Getty Images

Every reasonable effort has been made to contact the copyright holders, but if there are any errors or omissions, Hodder & Stoughton will be pleased to insert the appropriate acknowledgement in any subsequent printing of this publication.

All colour illustrations and chapter titles by Ellen Gregory McGrath © Anzu 2007. Ellen Gregory McGrath is a London-based illustrator with her own stationery company – Anzu (www.anzu.co.uk).